Rick Steves®

POCKET

LONDON

Rick Steves & Gene Openshaw

D0198128

Contents

Introduction

Blow through the city on a double-decker bus, and wander the lively West End. Hear the chimes of Big Ben, ogle the crown jewels at the Tower of London, and go for a spin on the London Eye. Visit with Van Gogh in the National Gallery, and rummage through our civilization's attic at the British Museum. Top off your day tipping a pint in a pub with a chatty local.

This is London. It's a city that seems perpetually at your service, with an impressive slate of sights, entertainment, and eateries, all linked by a great transit system. With a growing number of immigrants from all over the world, London has become a city of eight million separate dreams, learning—sometimes fitfully—to live as a microcosm of the once-vast British Empire.

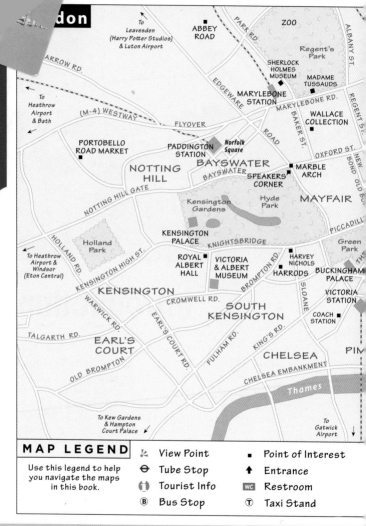

To
Leavesden
(Harry Potter Studios)
& Luton Airport

ABBEY
ROAD

ZOO

PARK RD.

Regent's
Park

ALBANY ST.

ARROW RD.

SHERLOCK
HOLMES
MUSEUM

MADAME
TUSSAUDS

To
Heathrow
Airport
& Bath

EDGEWARE

MARYLEBONE
STATION

MARYLEBONE RD.

REGENT ST.

BAKER ST.

(M-4) WESTWAY

FLYOVER

WALLACE
COLLECTION

ROAD

OXFORD ST.

NEW

BOND

OLD BO

PORTOBELLO
ROAD MARKET

PADDINGTON
STATION

Norfolk
Square

BAYSWATER

NOTTING
HILL

BAYSWATER

SPEAKERS
CORNER

MARBLE
ARCH

MAYFAIR

NOTTING HILL GATE

Kensington
Gardens

Hyde
Park

PICCADILL

HOLLAND RD.

Holland
Park

KENSINGTON
PALACE

KNIGHTSBRIDGE

Green
Park

TH

To Heathrow
Airport &
Windsor
(Eton Central)

KENSINGTON HIGH ST.

ROYAL
ALBERT
HALL

VICTORIA
& ALBERT
MUSEUM

BROMPTON RD.

HARVEY
NICHOLS

HARRODS

BUCKINGHAM
PALACE

KENSINGTON

WARWICK RD.

CROMWELL RD.

SOUTH
KENSINGTON

SLOANE

VICTORIA
STATION

TALGARTH RD.

EARL'S
COURT

EARL'S COURT RD.

FULHAM RD.

KING'S RD.

COACH
STATION

OLD BROMPTON

CHELSEA

PIM

To Kew Gardens
& Hampton
Court Palace

CHELSEA EMBANKMENT

Thames

To
Gatwick
Airport

MAP LEGEND

Use this legend to help
you navigate the maps
in this book.

	View Point	■	Point of Interest
⊖	Tube Stop	✦	Entrance
👫	Tourist Info	WC	Restroom
Ⓑ	Bus Stop	Ⓣ	Taxi Stand

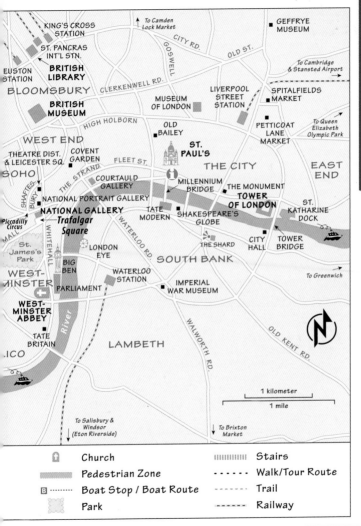

To Camden Lock Market
KING'S CROSS STATION
ST. PANCRAS INT'L STN.
EUSTON STATION
BRITISH LIBRARY
BLOOMSBURY
BRITISH MUSEUM
CITY RD.
GOSWELL
OLD ST.
GEFFRYE MUSEUM
To Cambridge & Stansted Airport
CLERKENWELL RD.
MUSEUM OF LONDON
LIVERPOOL STREET STATION
SPITALFIELDS MARKET
HIGH HOLBORN
OLD BAILEY
WEST END
THEATRE DIST. & LEICESTER SQ.
COVENT GARDEN
SOHO
SHAFTES-BURY
THE STRAND
FLEET ST.
PETTICOAT LANE MARKET
To Queen Elizabeth Olympic Park
ST. PAUL'S
THE CITY
EAST END
COURTAULD GALLERY
MILLENNIUM BRIDGE
THE MONUMENT
TOWER OF LONDON
ST. KATHARINE DOCK
NATIONAL PORTRAIT GALLERY
NATIONAL GALLERY
Trafalgar Square
Piccadilly Circus
MALL
WHITEHALL
TATE MODERN
SHAKESPEARE'S GLOBE
CITY HALL
TOWER BRIDGE
THE SHARD
St. James's Park
LONDON EYE
WATERLOO RD.
SOUTH BANK
To Greenwich
WEST-MINSTER
BIG BEN
PARLIAMENT
WATERLOO STATION
IMPERIAL WAR MUSEUM
WEST-MINSTER ABBEY
TATE BRITAIN
ICO
River
LAMBETH
WALWORTH RD.
OLD KENT RD.
N

1 kilometer
1 mile

To Salisbury & Windsor (Eton Riverside)
To Brixton Market

Symbol	Meaning	Symbol	Meaning
⛪	Church	‖‖‖	Stairs
▨	Pedestrian Zone	· · · · ·	Walk/Tour Route
B ····	Boat Stop / Boat Route	- - - -	Trail
▨	Park	----	Railway

About This Book

With this book, I've selected only the best of London—admittedly, a tough call. The core of the book is seven self-guided tours and walks. These zero in on London's greatest sights, from a Westminster Walk past #10 Downing Street, to the treasures of the British Library, to the glittering crown jewels at the Tower of London. The rest of the book is a traveler's tool kit. You'll find hints on saving money, avoiding crowds, getting around London, finding a great meal, and more.

If you'd like more information than this Pocket Guide offers, I've sprinkled the book liberally with web references. For general travel tips—as well as updates for this book—see **www.ricksteves.com.**

London—A City of Neighborhoods

London, with more than 600 square miles and eight million people, is a world in itself. On my first visit, I felt extremely small. But when you consider it as a collection of neighborhoods, London becomes manageable.

The River Thames runs roughly west to east through the city, with most sights on the north bank (in the area roughly enclosed by the Tube's Circle Line).

Key to This Book

Sights are rated:

▲▲▲ **Don't miss**
▲▲ **Try hard to see**
▲ **Worthwhile if you can make it**
No rating **Worth knowing about**

Tourist information offices are abbreviated as **TI,** and bathrooms are **WCs.**

Like Europe, this book uses the **24-hour clock.** It's the same through 12:00 noon, then keep going: 13:00 (1:00 p.m.), 14:00 (2:00 p.m.), and so on.

For **opening times,** if a sight is listed as "May-Oct daily 9:00-16:00," it's open from 9 a.m. until 4 p.m. from the first day of May until the last day of October.

London's Neighborhoods

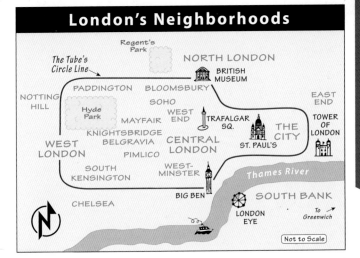

Central London: The heart of today's London contains the Westminster district (Big Ben, the Abbey, and #10 Downing Street) and the West End (Piccadilly Circus, theaters, restaurants, and nightlife). In the middle sits London's gathering place, Trafalgar Square.

The City: Surrounding St. Paul's Cathedral is the former walled city of Shakespeare's day. Now it's the modern financial district, called simply "The City." On its eastern border stands the Tower of London.

West London: This huge area surrounding the green expanse of Hyde Park/Kensington Gardens contains upscale neighborhoods such as Mayfair, Belgravia, Chelsea, South Kensington, and Notting Hill. Here you'll find a range of sights (Victoria and Albert Museum, Tate Britain, Harrods) and my top hotel recommendations.

North London: This contains the British Museum, the British Library, the overhyped Madame Tussauds Waxworks, and three major train stations.

The South Bank: The Thames' south bank offers major sights (Shakespeare's Globe, Tate Modern, London Eye) and minor attractions, all linked by a riverside walkway.

London at a Glance

▲▲▲**Westminster Abbey** Britain's finest church and the site of royal coronations and burials since 1066. **Hours:** Mon-Fri 9:30-16:30, Wed until 19:00, Sat 9:30-14:30, closed Sun to sightseers except for worship. See page 27.

▲▲▲**Churchill War Rooms** Underground WWII headquarters of Churchill's war effort. **Hours:** Daily 9:30-18:00. See page 124.

▲▲▲**National Gallery** Remarkable collection of European paintings (1250-1900), including Leonardo, Botticelli, Velázquez, Rembrandt, Turner, Van Gogh, and the Impressionists. **Hours:** Daily 10:00-18:00, Fri until 21:00. See page 39.

▲▲▲**British Museum** The world's greatest collection of artifacts of Western civilization, including the Rosetta Stone and the Parthenon's Elgin Marbles. **Hours:** Daily 10:00-17:30, Fri until 20:30 (selected galleries only). See page 71.

▲▲▲**British Library** Fascinating collection of the most important literary treasures of the Western world. **Hours:** Mon-Fri 9:30-18:00, Tue-Thu until 20:00, Sat 9:30-17:00, Sun 11:00-17:00. See page 97.

▲▲▲**St. Paul's Cathedral** The main cathedral of the Anglican Church, designed by Christopher Wren, with a climbable dome and daily evensong services. **Hours:** Mon-Sat 8:30-16:30, closed Sun except for worship. See page 138.

▲▲▲**Tower of London** Historic castle, palace, and prison housing the crown jewels and a witty band of Beefeaters. **Hours:** March-Oct Tue-Sat 9:00-17:30, Sun-Mon 10:00-17:30; Nov-Feb closes one hour earlier. See page 109.

▲▲▲**Victoria and Albert Museum** The best collection of decorative arts anywhere. **Hours:** Daily 10:00-17:45, Fri until 22:00 (selected galleries only). See page 152.

▲▲**Houses of Parliament** London's Neo-Gothic landmark, famous for Big Ben and occupied by the Houses of Lords and Commons. **Hours:** When Parliament is in session, generally open Mon-Thu, closed Fri-Sun and late July-Sept. Guided tours run Sat year-round plus weekdays during recess late July-Sept. See page 122.

▲▲**Trafalgar Square** The heart of London, where Westminster, The City, and the West End meet. **Hours:** Always open. See page 24.

▲▲**National Portrait Gallery** A *Who's Who* of British history, featuring portraits of this nation's most important historical figures. **Hours:** Daily 10:00-18:00, Thu-Fri until 21:00, first and second floors open Mon at 11:00. See page 126.

▲▲**Covent Garden** Vibrant people-watching zone with shops, cafés, street musicians, and an iron-and-glass arcade that once hosted a produce market. **Hours:** Always open. See page 64.

▲▲**Changing of the Guard at Buckingham Palace** Hour-long spectacle at Britain's royal residence. **Hours:** May-July daily at 11:00, Aug-April every other day. See page 131.

▲▲**London Eye** Enormous observation wheel, dominating—and offering commanding views over—London's skyline. **Hours:** Daily 10:00-20:30, later in July and Aug. See page 143.

▲▲**Imperial War Museum** Exhibits examining the military history of the bloody 20th century. **Hours:** Daily 10:00-18:00. See page 145.

▲▲**Tate Modern** Works by Monet, Matisse, Dalí, Picasso, and Warhol displayed in a converted powerhouse. **Hours:** Daily 10:00-18:00, Fri-Sat until 22:00. See page 146.

▲▲**Shakespeare's Globe** Timbered, thatched-roofed reconstruction of the Bard's original "wooden O." **Hours:** Theater complex, museum, and actor-led tours generally daily 9:00-17:00; in summer, morning theater tours only. Plays are also staged here. See page 147.

▲▲**Tate Britain** Collection of British painting from the 16th century through modern times, including works by William Blake, the Pre-Raphaelites, and J. M. W. Turner. **Hours:** Daily 10:00-18:00. See page 150.

▲▲**Kensington Palace** Recently restored former home of British monarchs, with appealing exhibits on Queen Victoria, as well as William and Mary. **Hours:** Daily 10:00-18:00, until 17:00 Nov-Feb. See page 153.

▲▲**Natural History Museum** Packed with stuffed creatures, engaging exhibits, and enthralled kids. **Hours:** Daily 10:00-18:00. See page 153.

▲**Courtauld Gallery** Fine collection of paintings filling one wing of the Somerset House, a grand 18th-century palace (may be closed when you visit). **Hours:** Daily 10:00-18:00. See page 128.

East London: East of The City is the once-grimy, increasingly gentri-fied East End. Even farther are the skyscraper-filled Docklands and Canary Wharf, plus Olympic Park—all newly developed areas signaling London's future.

Planning Your Time

The following day-plans give an idea of how much an organized, motivat-ed, and caffeinated person can see. Begin with the Day 1 plan—the most important sights—and add on from there.

Day 1: Start where London did, at the 950-year-old Tower of London, with its crown jewels, blustery Beefeaters, and bloody history. Pack a pic-nic lunch and cruise the Thames to Westminster Abbey; tour it and stay for the evensong. Then follow my self-guided Westminster Walk, ending with dinner in the West End.

Day 2: Take a London sightseeing bus tour and hop off at Buckingham Palace for the Changing of the Guard. After lunch, tour the Churchill War Rooms, and then the National Gallery. Have a pub dinner before a play, concert, or evening walking tour.

Day 3: Tour the British Museum and/or the British Library, then have lunch. Tube to Leicester Square to take my self-guided West End Walk: see Covent Garden and Soho, and browse the Regent Street shops. Enjoy afternoon tea at Fortnum & Mason or The Wolseley.

Day 4: Walk through The City and visit St. Paul's. Cross the Millennium Bridge to the South Bank of the Thames. Tour Shakespeare's Globe, the Tate Modern, and nearby sights. Then stroll the Jubilee Walkway to the London Eye.

Day 5: Explore a morning street market, especially Saturday at Portobello Road or Sunday at Spitalfields. Then choose from other major sights: Tate Britain, Museum of London, Imperial War Museum, or Kew Gardens.

Day 6: Tour the Victoria and Albert Museum, and/or its neighboring museums. Spend the afternoon strolling through Hyde Park or shopping at Harrods or other venues.

Day 7: Consider a day trip outside the city—a cruise to salty Greenwich, Hampton Palace, or Windsor Castle.

With More Time: Spend a day or two on side-trips to Cambridge, Stonehenge, or Bath.

Daily Reminder

Sunday: The Tower of London and British Museum are both especially crowded today. Speakers' Corner in Hyde Park rants from early afternoon until early evening. These places are closed: Sir John Soane's Museum and legal sights (Houses of Parliament, City Hall, and Old Bailey; the neighborhood called The City is dead). Westminster Abbey and St. Paul's are open during the day for worship but closed to sightseers. With all these closures, this morning is a good time to take a bus tour. Most big stores open late (around 11:30) and close early (18:00). Street markets flourish at Camden Lock, Spitalfields (at its best today), Petticoat Lane, Brick Lane, and Greenwich, but Portobello Road is closed. Most theaters (except maybe Shakespeare's Globe and *The Lion King*) are dark.

Monday: Nearly all sights are open, except Apsley House, Sir John Soane's Museum, and a few others. The Houses of Parliament may be open as late as 22:30.

Tuesday: Nearly all sights are open, except Apsley House. The British Library is open until 20:00, and the Houses of Parliament may be open as late as 22:00. On the first Tuesday of the month, Sir John Soane's Museum is also open until 21:00.

Wednesday: Nearly all sights are open. The British Library is open until 20:00 and the Houses of Parliament may be open as late as 22:00.

Thursday: All sights are open, the British Library is open until 20:00, and the National Portrait Gallery is open until 21:00.

Friday: All sights are open, except the Houses of Parliament. Sights open late include the British Museum (selected galleries until 20:30), National Gallery (until 21:00), National Portrait Gallery (until 21:00), Victoria and Albert Museum (selected galleries until 22:00), and Tate Modern (until 22:00).

Saturday: Most sights are open. The Old Bailey is closed. The Houses of Parliament are open only with a tour. Tate Modern is open until 22:00. The Tower of London is especially crowded today. The Portobello Road, Camden Lock, and Greenwich markets are good today.

These are busy day-plans, so be sure to schedule in slack time for laundry, people-watching, shopping, snafus, and recharging your touristic batteries.

Quick Tips: Here are a few quick sightseeing tips to get you started (✪ for more, see page 200). Master London's excellent public transportation system, and buy the right pass to make it economical. Use the "Daily Reminder" to visit sights at their most opportune time. Follow my tips on avoiding lines and crowds; consider getting advance tickets for a handful of big sights. ∩ Take advantage of my free London audio tours, covering many of this book's sights. Budget time and energy for London after dark. Dine well at least once.

And finally, keep in mind that London is more than its museums and landmarks. It's a living, breathing, thriving organism...a coral reef of humanity. Slow down and be open to unexpected experiences and the friendliness of the British people.

As you visit places I know and love, I'm happy you'll be meeting my favorite Londoners. Cheers!

Westminster Walk

From Big Ben to Trafalgar Square

Just about every visitor to London strolls along historic Whitehall from Big Ben to Trafalgar Square. Under London's modern traffic and big-city bustle lie 2,000 fascinating years of history. This quick nine-stop walk gives meaning to that touristy ramble.

As London's political center, the Westminster neighborhood is both historic and contemporary. See the River Thames where London was born. Pass statues and monuments to the nation's great heroes. Admire the Halls of Parliament where Britain is ruled today, and take a peek at #10 Downing Street, home of the prime minister. All in about an hour.

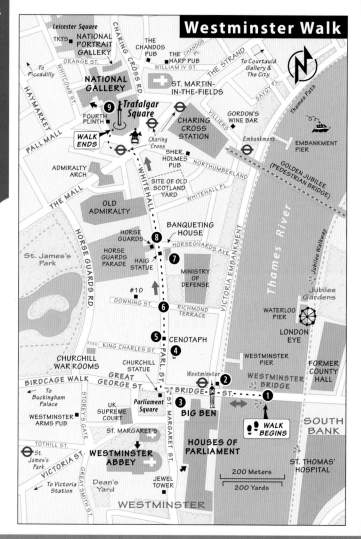

Westminster Walk

Leicester Square

TKTS

NATIONAL PORTRAIT GALLERY

CHARING CROSS RD.

ORANGE ST.

To Piccadilly

WHITCOMB ST.

NATIONAL GALLERY

HAYMARKET

FOURTH PLINTH

9 Trafalgar Square

WALK ENDS

PALL MALL

ADMIRALTY ARCH

THE MALL

OLD ADMIRALTY

HORSE GUARDS RD.

St. James's Park

THE CHANDOS PUB

THE CHANDOS PL.

HARP PUB

WILLIAM IV ST.

ST. MARTIN-IN-THE-FIELDS

Charing Cross

CHARING CROSS STATION

THE STRAND

To Courtauld Gallery & The City

SAVOY PL.

VILLIERS

GORDON'S WINE BAR

Embankment

Thames Path

EMBANKMENT PIER

SHER. HOLMES PUB

NORTHUMBERLAND

SITE OF OLD SCOTLAND YARD

WHITEHALL PL.

WHITEHALL

GOLDEN JUBILEE (PEDESTRIAN BRIDGE)

Thames River

HORSE GUARDS

8 BANQUETING HOUSE

HORSEGUARDS AVE.

HORSE GUARDS PARADE

HAIG STATUE

7

MINISTRY OF DEFENSE

VICTORIA EMBANKMENT

Jubilee Walkway

Jubilee Gardens

#10 DOWNING ST.

6

RICHMOND TERRACE

WATERLOO PIER

LONDON EYE

FORMER COUNTY HALL

KING CHARLES ST.

5 **4** CENOTAPH

PARL. ST.

CHURCHILL WAR ROOMS

CHURCHILL STATUE

BIRDCAGE WALK

GREAT GEORGE ST.

To Buckingham Palace

WESTMINSTER ARMS PUB

STOREY'S GATE

UK SUPREME COURT

Parliament Square

3 BIG BEN

Westminster

BRIDGE ST.

2

WESTMINSTER PIER

Westminster

WESTMINSTER BRIDGE

1

WALK BEGINS

SOUTH BANK

TOTHILL ST.

St. James's Park

VICTORIA ST.

To Victoria Station

GREAT SMITH ST.

ST. MARGARET'S

WESTMINSTER ABBEY

Dean's Yard

JEWEL TOWER

HOUSES OF PARLIAMENT

ST. THOMAS' HOSPITAL

200 Meters

200 Yards

WESTMINSTER

1. Westminster Bridge
2. Statue of Boadicea
3. View of Parliament Square
4. Walking Along Whitehall
5. Cenotaph
6. #10 Downing Street & Ministry of Defence
7. Banqueting House
8. Horse Guards
9. Trafalgar Square

ORIENTATION

Length of This Walk: Though the walk itself only takes an hour, you'll need more time if you decide to go inside sights along the way.

Getting There: Tube: Westminster, then take the Westminster Pier exit to Westminster Bridge.

WCs: Westminster Pier (pay); at the intersection of Bridge Street and Whitehall (underground, pay); and free WCs inside the Banqueting House, National Gallery, and St. Martin-in-the-Fields church.

Audio Tour: 🎧 Download my free Westminster Walk audio tour—see page 201.

Eateries: ✪ See page 176 for recommendations near Trafalgar Square.

THE WALK BEGINS

▶ *Start halfway across Westminster Bridge. Look upstream, toward Parliament.*

❶ On Westminster Bridge

Big Ben and the Houses of Parliament: Ding dong ding dong. Dong ding dong ding. Yes, indeed, you are in London.

Big Ben is actually "not the clock, not the tower, but the bell that tolls the hour." However, since the 13-ton bell is not visible, everyone just calls the whole works Big Ben. Named for a fat bureaucrat, Ben is scarcely older than my great-grandmother, but it has quickly become the city's symbol. The tower is 315 feet high, and the clock faces are 23 feet across. The 13-foot-long minute hand sweeps the length of your body every five minutes. For fun, call home from near Big Ben at about three minutes before the hour, to let your loved one hear the bell ring.

Big Ben is in the north tower of the Houses of Parliament, stretching

Big Ben—the clock face is 23 feet across   The Thames snakes through London to the sea.

along the Thames. Britain is ruled from this building, which for five centuries was the home of kings and queens. Then, as democracy was foisted on tyrants, a parliament of nobles was allowed to meet in some of the rooms. Soon, commoners were elected to office, the neighborhood was shot, and the royalty moved to Buckingham Palace. In 1834, the building was gutted by fire and rebuilt in the sandstone-hued, Neo-Gothic Parliament building we see today.

Today, the House of Commons meets in one end of the building. The rubber-stamp House of Lords grumbles and snoozes in the other end of this 1,000-room complex, and provides a tempering effect on extreme governmental changes. The two houses are very much separate: Notice the riverside tea terraces with the color-coded awnings—royal red for lords, common green for commoners. Alluding to the traditional leanings of the two chambers, locals say, "Green for go…red for stop." The modern Portcullis Building (with the tube-like chimneys), across Bridge Street from Big Ben, holds offices for the 650 members of the House of Commons. They commute to the Houses of Parliament by way of an underground passage.

The Thames: London's history is tied to the Thames, the 210-mile river linking the interior of England with the North Sea. The city got its start in Roman times as a trade center along this watery highway. As recently as a century ago, large ships made their way upstream to the city center to unload. Today, the major port is 25 miles downstream, and tourist cruise boats ply the waters.

Several tour-boat companies offer regular departures from Westminster Pier (on the left bank) or Waterloo Pier (on the right, near the London Eye). This is an efficient, scenic way to get to the Tower of London or Greenwich (downstream) or Kew Gardens (upstream).

For centuries, only London Bridge crossed the Thames. Then in 1750 Westminster Bridge was built. Early in the morning of September 3, 1802, William Wordsworth stood where you're standing and described what he saw:

> This City now doth, like a garment, wear
> The beauty of the morning; silent, bare,
> Ships, towers, domes, theatres, and temples lie
> Open unto the fields, and to the sky;
> All bright and glittering in the smokeless air.

You'll notice the **London Eye** on the South Bank, across the river. This 443-foot-tall Ferris wheel—originally nicknamed "the London Eyesore"—is now generally appreciated by locals, who see it as a welcome addition to their city's otherwise underwhelming skyline. Next to the wheel sprawls a carnival-like tourist complex. The London Eye marks the start of the Jubilee

The London Eye—built to celebrate the Millennium—proved so popular, they decided to keep it.

Walkway, a pleasant one-hour promenade along the vibrant, gentrified South Bank, with great views across the river.

▶ *Near Westminster Pier is a big statue of a lady on a chariot (nicknamed "the first woman driver"...no reins).*

❷ Statue of Boadicea, Queen of the Iceni

Riding in her two-horse chariot, daughters by her side, this Celtic Xena leads her people against Roman invaders. Julius Caesar was the first Roman general to cross the Channel, but even he was weirded out by the island's strange inhabitants, who worshipped trees, sacrificed virgins, and went to war painted blue.

Boadicea refused to be Romanized. In A.D. 60, after Roman soldiers raped her daughters, she rallied her people and massacred London's 60,000 Romanized citizens. However, the brief revolt was snuffed out, and she and her family took poison rather than surrender. The Romans civilized the Celts, building roads and making this spot on the Thames— "Londinium"—into a major urban center.

▶ *Cross the street to just under Big Ben and continue one block inland to the busy intersection of Parliament Square.*

❸ View of Parliament Square

To your left are the sandstone-hued **Houses of Parliament.** If Parliament is in session, the entrance (midway down the building) is lined with tourists, enlivened by political demonstrations, and staked out by camera crews interviewing Members of Parliament (MPs) for the evening news.

Kitty-corner across the square, the two white towers of **Westminster Abbey** rise above the trees. The cute little church with the blue sundials,

Boadicea—the Celts' last hurrah

Parliament Square and Westminster Abbey

snuggling under the Abbey "like a baby lamb under a ewe," is **St. Margaret's Church.** Since 1480, this has been the place for politicians' weddings, including Winston and Clementine Churchill's.

Parliament Square, the expanse of green between Westminster Abbey and Big Ben, is filled with statues of famous Brits such as **Winston Churchill,** the man who saved Britain from Hitler. According to tour guides, the statue has a current of electricity running through it to honor Churchill's wish that his head wouldn't be soiled by pigeons. A few non-Brits are honored for their contributions to mankind. **Nelson Mandela** (at the opposite corner of the square) battled South African apartheid, and **Abraham Lincoln** (far side of the square) opposed apartheid in America. The Lincoln statue, erected in 1920, was patterned after a similar statue in Chicago's Lincoln Park.

The broad boulevard of **Whitehall** (here called Parliament Street) stretches to your right up to Trafalgar Square. In 1868, this intersection became the site of a new innovation—the world's first traffic light.

▶ *Consider touring Westminster Abbey (✪ see the Westminster Abbey Tour on page 27) or the Houses of Parliament (✪ see page 122). Otherwise, turn right (north), and walk up Parliament Street, which becomes Whitehall.*

❹ Walking Along Whitehall

Today, Whitehall is choked with traffic, but imagine the effect this broad street must have had on out-of-towners a little over a century ago. In your horse-drawn carriage, you'd clop along a tree-lined boulevard—past well-dressed lords and ladies, dodging street urchins—your eyes dazzled by the bone-white walls of this man-made marble canyon.

Whitehall is now the most important street in Britain, lined with the ministries of finance, treasury, and so on. You may see limos and camera crews as important dignitaries enter or exit. Political demonstrators wave signs and chant slogans—sometimes about issues foreign to most Americans (Britain's former colonies resent the empire's continuing influence).

Notice the security measures. Iron grates seal off the concrete ditches between the buildings and sidewalks for protection against explosives. The city has been a target of terrorist attacks since long before September 2001, and Londoners take threats in stride.

▶ *Continue toward the tall, square, concrete monument in the middle of the road—the Cenotaph.*

Whitehall—government and monuments

Cenotaph—grim reminder of two World Wars

On your right is a colorful pub, the Red Lion. Across the street, a 700-foot detour down King Charles Street leads to the Churchill War Rooms (✪ see page 124), the underground bunker of 27 rooms that was the nerve center of Britain's campaign against Hitler.

❺ Cenotaph

This big, white stone monument (in the middle of the boulevard) honors those who died in the two events that most shaped modern Britain—World Wars I and II. The monumental devastation of these wars helped turn a colonial superpower into a cultural colony of an American superpower.

The actual cenotaph is the slab that sits atop the pillar—a tomb. You'll notice no religious symbols on this memorial. The dead honored here came from many creeds and all corners of Britain's empire. It looks lost in a sea of noisy cars, but on each Remembrance Sunday (closest to November 11), Whitehall is closed off to traffic, the royal family fills the balcony overhead in the foreign ministry, and a memorial service is held around the cenotaph.

It's hard for an American to understand the impact of World War I on Europe (1914-1918). On a single day, the British suffered nearly 60,000 casualties. It's said that if the roughly one million WWI dead from the British Empire were to march four abreast past the cenotaph, the sad parade would last for seven days.

▶ *Just past the cenotaph, on the west side of Whitehall, is an iron security gate guarding the entrance to Downing Street.*

❻ #10 Downing Street and the Ministry of Defense

Britain's version of the White House is where the prime minister and his family live, at #10. It's in the black-brick building 300 feet down the blocked-off street, on the right; there's a lantern and usually a security guard.

Like the White House's Rose Garden, the black door marked #10 is a highly symbolic point of power, popular for photo ops to mark big occasions. This is where suffragettes protested in the early 20th century, where Neville Chamberlain showed off his regrettable peace treaty with Hitler, where Winston Churchill made famous the V-for-Victory sign, and where former President Barack Obama came to discuss economic policy.

It looks modest, but #10's entryway does open up into fairly impressive digs—the prime minister's offices (downstairs), his residence (upstairs), and two large formal dining rooms. The PM's staff has offices here. Many on the staff are permanent bureaucrats, staying on to serve as prime ministers come and go. The cabinet meets at #10 on Tuesday mornings. This is where foreign dignitaries are wined and dined, where the prime minister receives honored schoolkids and victorious soccer teams, and where he gives monthly addresses to the nation. Next door, at #11, the chancellor of the exchequer (finance minister) lives with his family, and at #12 is the PM's press office.

This has been the traditional home of the prime minister since the position was created in the early 18th century. But even before that, the neighborhood (if not the building itself) was a center of power, where Edward the Confessor and Henry VIII had palaces. The facade is, frankly, quite cheap, having been built as part of a middle-class cul-de-sac of homes by Dublin-born George Downing in the 1680s. When the first PM moved in, the humble interior was combined with a mansion in back. During a major upgrade in the 1950s, they discovered that the facade's black bricks were actually

Heavy security for #10 Downing Street

Memorial to WWII women

yellow—but had been stained by centuries of Industrial Age soot. To keep with tradition, they now paint the bricks black.

The guarded metal gates were installed in 1989 to protect against Irish terrorists. Even so, #10 was hit and partly damaged in 1991 by an Irish Republican Army mortar launched from a van. These days, there's typically not much to see unless a VIP happens to drive up. Then the bobbies snap to and check credentials, the gates open, the car is inspected for bombs, the traffic barrier midway down the street drops into its bat cave, the car drives in, and...the bobbies go back to mugging for the tourists.

The huge building across Whitehall from Downing Street is the **Ministry of Defence** (MOD), the "British Pentagon." This bleak place looks like a Ministry of Defence should. In front, statues honor illustrious defenders of Britain, including **Field Marshal Bernard Law Montgomery ("Monty")** who beat the Nazis in North Africa. A **memorial** honoring the women who fought and died in World War II stands in the middle of the street.

You may be enjoying the shade of London's **plane trees.** Their bark sheds and regenerates, which helps them survive in polluted London.

▶ *Continue up Whitehall to the equestrian statue in the middle of the street. On the right side of Whitehall is the Banqueting House.*

❼ Banqueting House

This two-story building is just about all that remains of what was once the biggest palace in Europe—Whitehall Palace, which stretched from Trafalgar Square to Big Ben. Henry VIII started the building, and Queen Elizabeth I and other monarchs added on as England's worldwide prestige grew. Then in 1698, a massive fire destroyed Whitehall Palace, leaving only its former dining hall, the Banqueting House.

Today, the exterior of Greek-style columns and pediments looks rather ho-hum, much like every other white, marble building in London. But when it was built in 1620 by architect Inigo Jones, it was the first of its kind, rising above half-timbered thatched buildings. Within a century, London was awash in Georgian-style architecture, the English version of Neoclassical.

The Banqueting House was the site of one of the pivotal events of English history. On January 30, 1649, a man dressed in black stepped out one of the windows and onto a wooden platform. It was King Charles I. He gave a short speech to a huge crowd assembled outside. Then he knelt and laid his neck on a block as another man in black approached. It was

Banqueting House—Neoclassical trendsetter

Horse Guard manning a symbolic checkpoint

the executioner—who cut off the King's head. Plop—the concept of divine monarchy in Britain was decapitated. Though the monarchy was restored a generation later, every ruler since then knows that the monarchy reigns by the grace of Parliament.

▶ *If you're interested in touring the impressive Banqueting House interior,* ✪ *see page 125. Otherwise, continue up Whitehall on the left (west) side, where you'll see (and smell) the building known as Horse Guards, guarded by traditionally dressed soldiers who are also called Horse Guards.*

❽ Horse Guards

For 200 years, soldiers in cavalry uniforms have guarded this arched entrance along Whitehall. Back when the archway was the only access point to The Mall (the street leading to Buckingham Palace), it was a crucial security checkpoint. By tradition, it's still guarded with much pomp and fanfare.

Two different squads alternate, so depending on the day you visit, you'll see soldiers in either red coats with white plumes in their helmets (the Life Guards), or blue coats with red plumes (the Blues and Royals). Together, they constitute the Queen's personal bodyguard. Besides their ceremonial duties here in old-time uniforms, these elite troops have fought in recent wars in Iraq and Afghanistan. Both Prince William and Prince Harry have served in the Blues and Royals.

The Horse Guards building was the headquarters of the British army from the time of the American Revolution until the Ministry of Defence was created in World War II. Through the arch is the broad expanse of the Horse Guards Parade, where troops parade to honor the monarch's birthday (Changing of the Guard is Mon-Sat at 10:30, Sun at 9:30, dismounting

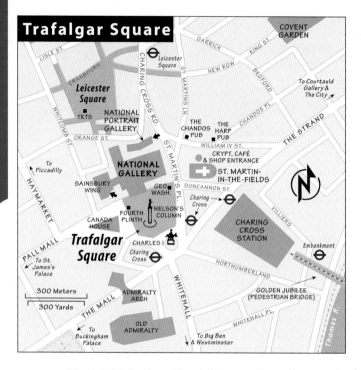

ceremony daily at 16:00; the Horse Guards Museum offers a glimpse at the stables and a collection of uniforms and weapons).

▶ *Continue up Whitehall, passing the Old Admiralty (#26, on left), head-quarters of the British navy that once ruled the waves. Across the street, behind the old Clarence Pub, stood the original Scotland Yard, headquarters of London's crack police force in the days of Sherlock Holmes. Finally, Whitehall opens up into the grand noisy, traffic-filled Trafalgar Square.*

❾ Trafalgar Square

London's central meeting point bustles around the world's biggest Corinthian column, where **Admiral Horatio Nelson** stands 185 feet off the ground, looking over London in the direction of one of the greatest naval battles in history. Nelson saved England at a time as dark as World War II. In 1805, Napoleon was poised on the other side of the Channel, threatening to invade England. Meanwhile, more than 900 miles away, the one-armed, one-eyed, and one-minded Lord Nelson attacked the French fleet off the coast of Spain at Trafalgar. The French were routed, Britannia ruled the waves, and the once-invincible French army was slowly worn down, then defeated at Waterloo. Nelson, while victorious, was shot by a sniper in the battle. He died, gasping, "Thank God, I have done my duty."

At the base of Nelson's column are bronze reliefs cast from melted-down enemy cannons, and four huggable lions dying to have their photo taken with you. In front of the column is a statue of Charles I on horseback, with his head still on his shoulders. In the pavement just behind the statue is a plaque marking the center of London, from which all distances are measured. Of the many statues that dot the square, the pedestal on the northwest corner (the "fourth plinth") is periodically topped with contemporary art. The newly restored fountains, lit by colored lights, can shoot

Trafalgar Square—full of fountains, people, and statues—is the thriving center of the city.

water 80 feet in the air. At the top of Trafalgar Square (north) sits the domed **National Gallery** with its grand staircase, and, to the right, the steeple of **St. Martin-in-the-Fields,** built in 1722, inspiring the steeple-over-the-entrance style of many town churches in New England.

Trafalgar Square is indeed the center of modern London, connecting Westminster, The City, and the West End. Spin clockwise 360 degrees and survey the city:

- To the south lies Westminster. Buckingham Palace is to the southwest, down the broad boulevard called The Mall.

- Leicester Square, Piccadilly Circus, and Soho are a few blocks north-northwest of Trafalgar Square.

- The area called The City—London's oldest section and today's financial district—is a mile northeast of Trafalgar Square, up the boulevard called the Strand.

- And finally, Northumberland Street leads southeast to the Golden Jubilee pedestrian bridge over the Thames.

Soak it in. You're smack-dab in the center of London, a thriving city atop two millennia of history.

Westminster Abbey Tour

Westminster Abbey is the most famous English church in Christendom, where the nation's royalty has been wedded, crowned, and buried since the 11th century. The histories of Westminster Abbey and England are almost the same. A thousand years of English history (and 3,000 tombs) lie within its stained-glass splendor and under its stone slabs.

On this hour-plus walk, we'll stroll through the elaborate Gothic architecture of the church and see some of England's dearly departed, including the tombs of 29 kings and queens. We'll see memorials to England's greatest politicians, scientists, writers, and warriors. And—in the heart of the church—we'll visit the spot where, one fine day, Prince Charles (or William or little George) will be crowned the next King of England.

Rick Steves | Pocket London

ORIENTATION

Cost: £20, £40 family ticket (2 adults and 1 child), includes fine audioguide and entry to the cloister.

Hours: Abbey—Mon-Fri 9:30-16:30, Wed until 19:00 (main church only), Sat 9:30-14:30, last entry one hour before closing, closed Sun to sightseers but open for services; cloister—daily 8:00-18:00.

Avoiding Lines: The Abbey is especially crowded midmorning, and all day Sat and Mon. Visit early, during lunch, or after 14:30 (then stay for the 17:00 evensong). From April through September you can skip the line by booking tickets in advance via the Abbey's website.

Dress Code: None, even for services.

Getting There: Near Big Ben and the Houses of Parliament (Tube: Westminster or St. James's Park).

Information: Because special events can shut out sightseers, check the website or call ahead for the latest on opening hours, guided tours, and concerts. At the cathedral, robed marshals are helpful. Tel. 020/7222-5152, www.westminster-abbey.org.

Church Services and Music: Mon-Fri at 7:30 (prayer), 8:00 (communion), 12:30 (communion), 17:00 evensong (except on Wed); Sat and Sun evensong at 15:00 (except May-Aug, when it's 17:00); full day of services on Sun—see website. Worship is free but no sightseeing during services. Free organ recitals many Sundays at 17:45.

Tours: The included audioguide is excellent. Entertaining 90-minute, £5 guided tours leave up to six times daily from the entrance.

WCs: Inside the Abbey, WCs are in the cloister and next to the café. Outside the abbey, the nearest public WCs (pay) are in front of Methodist Central Hall, the domed building across the street from the Abbey's west entrance.

Photography: Photos are prohibited, except in the Little Cloister and College Garden.

Cuisine Art: There's a $$ café in the cellar. Outside the Abbey, find cafeteria-style lunches at $ Wesley's Café inside Methodist Central Hall (daily 9:00-16:00). $$ The Westminster Arms pub (£10 fish and chips, food served daily 12:00-20:00) is near Methodist Central Hall on Storey's Gate. Picnickers can find benches at the nearby Jewel Tower, a half-block south of the Abbey.

Starring: Edwards, Elizabeths, Henrys, Annes, Marys, and poets.

THE TOUR BEGINS

You'll have no choice but to follow the steady flow of tourists on a one-way circuit through the church, following the route laid out for the audioguide. Most days the crowds can be a real crush. Here are the Abbey's top 10 (plus one) stops.

▶ *Walk straight in, entering the north transept. Pick up the free map/flier and audioguide. Follow the crowd flow to the right, passing through* **"Scientists' Corner,"** *with memorials to Isaac Newton, Michael Faraday, Charles Darwin, and others. Enter the spacious...*

❶ Nave

Look down the long and narrow center aisle of the church. Lined with the praying hands of the Gothic arches, glowing with light from the stained glass, this is more than a museum. With saints in stained glass, heroes in carved stone, and the bodies of England's greatest citizens under the floor stones, Westminster Abbey is the religious heart of England.

The Abbey was built in 1065. Its name, Westminster, means Church in the West (west of St. Paul's Cathedral). The king who built the Abbey was Edward the Confessor. Find him in the stained glass windows on the left side of the nave ("left" as you face the altar). He's in the third bay from the end (marked **S: Edwardus rex...**), with his crown, scepter, and ring. Take some time to thank him for this Abbey.

The Abbey's 10-story nave is the tallest in England. The chandeliers, 10 feet tall, look small in comparison (16 were given to the Abbey by the Guinness family).

On the floor near the west entrance of the Abbey is the flower-lined

Memorials to Great Britons in the nave

Crisscross vaults in this medieval church

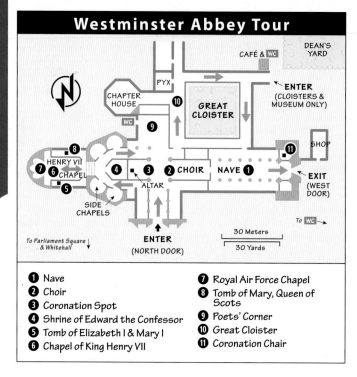

Westminster Abbey Tour

DEAN'S YARD

CAFÉ & WC

PYX

ENTER (CLOISTERS & MUSEUM ONLY)

CHAPTER HOUSE

WC

GREAT CLOISTER

⓾

⑨

⑧ HENRY VII CHAPEL

⑦ ⑥

⑤

④

③

② CHOIR

NANE ①

⑪ SHOP

EXIT (WEST DOOR)

ALTAR

SIDE CHAPELS

To Parliament Square & Whitehall

ENTER (NORTH DOOR)

30 Meters

30 Yards

To WC

❶ Nave
❷ Choir
❸ Coronation Spot
❹ Shrine of Edward the Confessor
❺ Tomb of Elizabeth I & Mary I
❻ Chapel of King Henry VII

❼ Royal Air Force Chapel
❽ Tomb of Mary, Queen of Scots
❾ Poets' Corner
❿ Great Cloister
⓫ Coronation Chair

Grave of the Unknown Warrior, one ordinary WWI soldier buried in soil from France with lettering made from melted-down weapons. Contemplate the million-man army from the British Empire, and all those who gave their lives. Their memory is so revered that, when Kate Middleton walked up the aisle on her wedding day, by tradition she had to step around the tomb. Hanging on a column next to the tomb is the US Medal of Honor, presented by General John J. Pershing in 1921 to honor England's WWI dead. Closer to the door is a memorial to a hero of World War II, Winston Churchill.

▶ *Now walk straight up the nave toward the altar. This is the same route every future monarch walks on the way to being crowned. Midway up*

The wooden seats of the choir—nestled in the spacious nave—are for clergy and singers.

the nave, you pass through the colorful screen of an enclosure known as the...

❷ Choir

These elaborately carved wood and gilded seats are where monks once chanted their services in the "quire"—as it's known in British churchspeak. Today, it's where the Abbey boys' choir sings the evensong. You're approaching the center of a cross-shaped church. The **"high" (main) altar** (which usually has a cross and candlesticks atop it) sits on the platform up the five stairs in front of you. It's on this platform that the monarch is crowned.

❸ Coronation Spot

The area immediately before the high altar is where every English coronation since 1066 has taken place. Imagine the day when Prince Charles or Prince William becomes king.

The nobles in robes and powdered wigs look on from the carved wooden stalls of the choir. The Archbishop of Canterbury stands at the high altar. The coronation chair (which we'll see later) is placed before the altar on the round, brown pavement stone representing the earth. Surrounding the whole area are temporary bleachers for 8,000 VIPs, going halfway up the rose windows of each transept, creating a "theater."

Long silver trumpets hung with banners sound a fanfare as the monarch-to-be enters the church. The congregation sings, "I will go into the house of the Lord," as William parades slowly down the nave and up the steps to the altar. After a church service, he sits in the chair, facing the altar, where the crown jewels are placed. William is anointed with holy oil, and then receives a ceremonial sword, ring, and cup. The royal scepter is placed in his hands, and—dut, dutta dah—the archbishop lowers the Crown of St. Edward the Confessor onto his royal head. Finally, King William V stands up, descends the steps, and is presented to the people. As cannons roar throughout the city, the people cry, "God save the king!"

The Abbey is also the place for royal funerals (Princess Diana in 1997, the Queen's mother in 2002) and for weddings (Queen Elizabeth II and Prince Philip in 1947). In 2011, Prince William and Kate Middleton strolled up the nave, passed through the choir, climbed the five steps to the high altar, and became husband and wife—and the future King and Queen of the United Kingdom and its Commonwealth. Though royal marriages and funerals can happen anywhere, only one church can hold a coronation—the Abbey.

▶ *Now veer left and follow the crowd. You'll walk past the statue of Robert ("Bob") Peel, the prime minister whose policemen were nicknamed "bobbies." Stroll a few yards into the land of dead kings and queens. Use the audioguide to explore the **side chapels**—the Chapel of St. John the Baptist and Chapel of St. Michael. There you'll see effigies of the dead lying atop their tombs of polished stone. They lie on their backs or recline on their sides. Dressed in ruffed collars, they relax on pillows, clasping their hands in prayer, many buried side by side with their spouse.*

After exploring the chapels, pause at the wooden staircase on your right.

❹ Shrine of Edward the Confessor

The holiest part of the church is the raised area behind the altar (where the wooden staircase leads—sorry, no tourist access except with verger tour). Step back and peek over the dark coffin of Edward I to see the tippy-top of the green-and-gold wedding-cake tomb of King Edward the Confessor—the man who built Westminster Abbey. It was finished just in time to bury Edward and to crown his foreign successor, William the Conqueror, in 1066.

▶ *Continue on. At the top of the stone staircase, veer left into the private burial chapel of Queen Elizabeth I.*

❺ Tomb of Queens Elizabeth I and Mary I

Although there's only one effigy on the tomb (Elizabeth's), there are actually two queens buried beneath it, both daughters of Henry VIII (by different mothers). Bloody Mary—meek, pious, sickly, and Catholic—enforced Catholicism during her short reign (1553-1558) by burning "heretics" at the stake.

Elizabeth—strong, clever, and Protestant—steered England on an Anglican course. She holds a royal orb symbolizing that she's queen of the whole globe. When 26-year-old Elizabeth was crowned in the Abbey, her right to rule was questioned because she was considered the bastard seed of Henry VIII's unsanctioned marriage to Anne Boleyn. But Elizabeth's long reign (1559-1603) was one of the greatest in English history, a time when England ruled the seas and Shakespeare explored human emotions. When she died, thousands turned out for her funeral in the Abbey. Elizabeth's face on the tomb, modeled after her death mask, is considered

Elizabeth I, buried alongside her sister and rival   Chapel of King Henry VII—exuberant Gothic

a very accurate take on this hook-nosed, imperious "Virgin Queen" (she never married).

The two half-sisters disliked each other in life—Mary even had Elizabeth locked up in the Tower of London for a short time. Now they lie side by side for eternity. The Latin inscription ends, "Here we lie, two sisters in hope of one resurrection."

▸ *Continue into the ornate, flag-draped room behind the main altar.*

❻ Chapel of King Henry VII (The Lady Chapel)

The light from the stained-glass windows; the colorful banners overhead; and the elaborate tracery in stone, wood, and glass give this room the festive air of a medieval tournament. The prestigious Knights of the Bath meet here, under the magnificent ceiling studded with gold pendants. The ceiling—of carved stone, not plaster (1519)—is a textbook example of English Perpendicular Gothic and fan vaulting. The ceiling was sculpted on the floor in pieces, then jigsaw-puzzled into place.

The knights sit in the wooden stalls with their coats of arms on the back, churches on their heads, their banner flying above, and the graves of dozens of kings beneath their feet. When the Queen worships here, she sits in the southwest corner chair under the carved wooden throne with the lion crown.

Behind the small altar is an iron cage housing the tombs of Henry VII of Lancaster and Elizabeth of York, whose marriage finally settled the Wars of the Roses between those two clans. Henry VII, the first Tudor king, was the father of Henry VIII and the grandfather of Elizabeth I. This exuberant chapel heralds a new optimistic, postwar era as England prepares to step onto the world stage.

▸ *At the far end of the chapel is a modern set of stained-glass windows.*

❼ Royal Air Force Chapel

Saints in robes and halos mingle with pilots in parachutes and bomber jackets. This tribute to WWII flyers is for those who earned their angel wings in the Battle of Britain (July–Oct 1940). When Hitler's air force threatened to snuff Britain out without a fight, British pilots stepped up. These were the fighters about whom Churchill said, "Never...was so much owed by so many to so few."

The Abbey survived the Battle and the Blitz, but this window did not, so it was replaced with this modern memorial. The book of remembrances lists each of the 1,497 airmen (including one American) who died in the Battle of Britain.

▸ *Exit the Chapel of Henry VII. Turn left into a side chapel with the tomb (the central one of three in the chapel).*

❽ Tomb of Mary, Queen of Scots

Historians get dewy-eyed over the fate of Mary, Queen of Scots (1542–1587). The beautiful ruler of Scotland (then an independent country) was executed for treason by her cousin, Queen Elizabeth I. After Elizabeth died childless, Mary's son—James VI, King of Scots—also became King James I of England and Ireland. James honored his mum with the Abbey's most sumptuous tomb.

▸ *Exit Mary's chapel. Ahead of you, again, is the tomb of the church's founder, Edward the Confessor. Continue on, until you emerge in the south transept. You're in Poets' Corner.*

❾ Poets' Corner

England's greatest artistic contributions are in the written word. Here the masters of arguably the world's most complex and expressive language are remembered. (Many writers are honored with plaques and monuments; relatively few are actually buried here.)

▸ *Start with Chaucer, buried in the wall under the blue windows, marked with a white plaque reading* Qui Fuit Anglorum...

Geoffrey Chaucer (c. 1343-1400) is often considered the father of English literature. Chaucer's **Canterbury Tales** told of earthy people speaking everyday English. He was the first great writer buried in the Abbey (thanks to his job as a Westminster clerk). Later, it became a tradition to bury other writers here, and Poets' Corner was built around his tomb. The blue windows have blank panels awaiting the names of future poets.

▶ *The plaques on the floor before Chaucer are gravestones and memorials to other literary greats, including ....*

Lord Byron, the great lover of women and adventure: "Though the night was made for loving, / And the day returns too soon, / Yet we'll go no more a-roving / By the light of the moon."

Dylan Thomas, alcoholic master of modernism, with a Romantic's heart: "Oh as I was young and easy in the mercy of his means, / Time held me green and dying / Though I sang in my chains like the sea."

Alfred, Lord Tennyson, conscience of the Victorian era: "'Tis better to have loved and lost / Than never to have loved at all."

Robert Browning: "Oh, to be in England / Now that April's there."

▶ *Farther out in the south transept, you'll find a statue of...*

William Shakespeare: Although he's not buried here, this greatest of English writers is honored by a fine statue that stands near the end of the transept, overlooking the others: "Life's but a walking shadow, a poor player that struts and frets his hour upon the stage and then is heard no more."

George Frideric Handel: High on the wall opposite Shakespeare is the German immigrant famous for composing the **Messiah** oratorio: "Hallelujah, hallelujah, hallelujah." His actual tomb is on the floor, next to...

Shakespeare's memorial in Poets' Corner: "I would give all my fame for a pot of ale…"

The cloister—covered walkways for monks

Coronation chair with slot for Stone of Scone

Charles Dickens, whose serialized novels brought literature to the masses: "It was the best of times, it was the worst of times."

And finally, near the center of the transept, find the small, white floor plaque of **Thomas Parr** (marked *THO: PARR*). Check the dates of his life (1483-1635) and do the math. In his (reputed) 152 years, he served 10 sovereigns and was a contemporary of Columbus, Henry VIII, Elizabeth I, Shakespeare, and Galileo.

▶ *Exit the church (temporarily) at the south door, which leads to the...*

⑩ Great Cloister

The buildings that adjoin the church once housed monks. (The church is known as the "abbey" because it was the headquarters of the Benedictine Order until Henry VIII kicked them out in 1540.) Cloistered courtyards gave them a place to meditate on God's creations. The cloister also has fine views of the flying buttresses that support the church walls, which allowed Gothic architects to build so high.

The **Chapter House** is where the monks had daily meetings. It features fine architecture and stained glass, some faded but well-described medieval paintings and floor tiles, and—in the corridor—Britain's oldest door. A few steps farther down the hall is the **Pyx Chamber,** which once safeguarded the coins used to set the silver standard of the realm.

▶ *Go back into the church for the last stop.*

⑪ Coronation Chair

A gold-painted oak chair waits here under a regal canopy for the next coronation. For every English coronation since 1308 (except two), it's been moved to its spot before the high altar to receive the royal buttocks. The chair's legs rest on lions, England's symbol. The space below the chair originally held a big sandstone rock from Scotland called the Stone of Scone (pronounced "skoon"), symbolizing Scotland's unity with England's monarch. But in the 1990s, Britain gave Scotland more sovereignty, its own Parliament, and the Stone, which Scotland has agreed to loan to Britain for future coronations (the rest of the time, it's on display in Edinburgh Castle).

Next to the chapel with the chair hangs a 600-year-old portrait of King Richard II. The boy king is holding the royal orb and scepter, wearing the crown, and seated upon this very chair.

Finally, take one last look down the nave. Listen to and ponder this place, filled with the remains of the people who made Britain a world power—saints, royalty, poets, musicians, scientists, soldiers, politicians. Now step back outside into a city filled with modern-day poets, saints, and heroes who continue to make Britain great.

National Gallery Tour

The National Gallery lets you tour Europe's art without ever crossing the Channel. Britain's best collection of paintings features all the biggies: Leonardo da Vinci, Rembrandt, Monet, Van Gogh, and more. With so many exciting artists and styles, it's a fine overture to art if you're just starting a European trip, and a pleasant reprise if you're just finishing. The "National Gal" is always a welcome interlude from the bustle of London sightseeing.

In this 90-minute tour we'll travel chronologically through art history: from medieval holiness to Renaissance realism, from Dutch detail to Baroque bombast, from British restraint to the colorful French Impressionism that leads to the modern world. We'll cruise like an eagle with wide eyes for the big picture, seeing how each style progresses into the next.

MEDIEVAL & EARLY RENAISSANCE

1 ANONYMOUS – The Wilton Diptych
2 UCCELLO – Battle of San Romano
3 VAN EYCK – The Arnolfini Portrait

ITALIAN RENAISSANCE

4 LEONARDO – The Virgin of the Rocks
5 BOTTICELLI – Venus and Mars
6 CRIVELLI – The Annunciation, with Saint Emidius

HIGH RENAISSANCE & MANNERISM

7 LEONARDO – Virgin and Child with St. Anne and St. John the Baptist
8 MICHELANGELO – The Entombment
9 RAPHAEL – Pope Julius II
10 BRONZINO – An Allegory with Venus and Cupid
11 TINTORETTO – The Origin of the Milky Way

NORTHERN PROTESTANT ART

12 VERMEER – A Young Woman Standing at a Virginal
13 VAN HOOGSTRATEN – A Peepshow with Views of the Interior of a Dutch House
14 REMBRANDT – Belshazzar's Feast
15 REMBRANDT – Self-Portrait at the Age of 63

BAROQUE & FRENCH ROCOCO

16 RUBENS – The Judgment of Paris
17 VELÁZQUEZ – The Rokeby Venus
18 VAN DYCK – Equestrian Portrait of Charles I
19 CARAVAGGIO –The Supper at Emmaus
20 BOUCHER – Pan and Syrinx

To Leicester Square ⊖
(5 min. walk)

SAINSBURY WING

ENTRANCE ON LEVEL 0

SELF-GUIDED TOUR
STARTS ON LEVEL 2

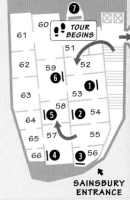

SAINSBURY
ENTRANCE

BRITISH ROMANTIC ART

21 CONSTABLE – The Hay Wain
22 TURNER – The Fighting Téméraire

National Gallery

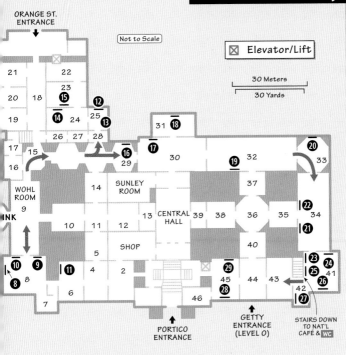

ORANGE ST.
ENTRANCE

Not to Scale

⊠ Elevator/Lift

30 Meters
30 Yards

21 22
23
20 18 ⑮
19 ⑭ 24 25 ⑫ ⑬
26 27 28
17 15
16 ⑯ 29 ⑰ 31 ⑱ ⑳ 33
WOHL 30 32
ROOM 14 SUNLEY 37 ⑲ ㉒
9 ROOM 13 CENTRAL 39 38 36 35 34 ㉑
INK 10 11 12 HALL 40
5 SHOP ㉙ 45 44 43 ㉓ ㉔ ㉕ ㉖ 41
⑩ ⑨ ㉘ 42 ㉗
⑧ 8 ⑪ 4 2 46
6
7

PORTICO
ENTRANCE

GETTY
ENTRANCE
(LEVEL O)

STAIRS DOWN
TO NAT'L
CAFÉ & WC

Trafalgar Square NELSON'S
COLUMN

To Charing Cross
(2 min. walk) →

IMPRESSIONISM & BEYOND

㉓ MONET – Gare St. Lazare
㉔ MONET – The Water-Lily Pond
㉕ MANET – Corner of a Café-Concert
㉖ SEURAT – Bathers at Asnières

㉗ RENOIR – The Skiff
㉘ VAN GOGH – Sunflowers
㉙ CÉZANNE – Bathers

ORIENTATION

Cost: Free, but £20 suggested donation. Special exhibits require an admission fee.

Hours: Daily 10:00-18:00, Fri until 21:00, last entry to special exhibits 45 minutes before closing.

Getting There: It's central as can be, overlooking Trafalgar Square (Tube: Charing Cross or Leicester Square). Handy buses #9, #11, #15, and #24 (among others) pass by.

Information: Tel. 020/7747-2885, switchboard tel. 020/7839-3321, www.nationalgallery.org.uk.

Tours: Free one-hour tours leave from the Sainsbury Wing info desk daily at 11:30 and 14:30, plus Fri at 19:00 and Sat-Sun at 16:00. The excellent £4 audioguides offer an array of tours, including one that lets you dial up info on any painting.

Cloakroom: Located at each entrance (£1 for bags). You can take a small bag into the museum.

Photography: Photos are allowed without flash.

Cuisine Art: There are three eateries in the Gallery. The $$$ National Dining Rooms—located on the first floor of the Sainsbury Wing—has a classy, table-service restaurant menu. The $$$ National Café—located near the Getty Entrance—has a table-service restaurant and an adjoining $ sandwich/soup/salad/pastry buffet. The $ Espresso Bar, also near the Getty Entrance, has soft couches and sandwiches. Outside the Gallery, there are several options near Trafalgar Square (✪ see page 176).

THE TOUR BEGINS

The Gallery has three entrances facing Trafalgar Square. Our tour starts from the Sainsbury Entrance, located far to the left of the central dome. The paintings are all on one floor. To see the art in chronological order requires a bit of map-reading and navigating, but it's worth it.

▶ *Enter through the Sainsbury Entrance. Pick up the handy map (£1) and climb the stairs. At the top, turn left, then left again, entering Room 52.*

Medieval and Early Renaissance (1200s-Early 1400s)

In Rooms 52 and 53, you see shiny gold paintings of saints, angels, Madonnas, and crucifixions float in an ethereal gold never-never land. One thing is very clear: Medieval heaven was different from medieval earth. The holy wore gold plates on their heads. Faces were serene and generic. People posed stiffly, facing directly out or to the side, never in between. Saints are recognized by the symbols they carry (a key, a sword, a book), rather than by their human features.

Art in the Middle Ages was religious, dominated by the Church. The illiterate faithful could meditate on an altarpiece and visualize heaven. It's as though they couldn't imagine saints and angels inhabiting the dreary world of rocks, trees, and sky they lived in.

▶ *One of the finest medieval altarpieces is in a glass case in Room 53.*

❶ Anonymous—*The Wilton Diptych* (c. 1395-1399)

Three kings (left panel) come to adore Mary and her rosy-cheeked baby (right panel), surrounded by flame-like angels. The kings have expressive faces, and the back side shows a deer in the grass. Still, the anonymous artist is struggling with reality. The figures are flat, scrawny, and sinless. Mary's exquisite fingers hold an anatomically impossible little foot. John the Baptist (among the kings) is holding a "lamb of God" that looks more like a Chihuahua. Nice try.

▶ *Continuing into Room 54, you'll leave this gold-leaf peace and find...*

❷ Uccello—*Battle of San Romano* (c. 1438-1440)

This colorful battle scene shows the victory of Florence over Siena—and the battle for literal realism on the canvas. It's an early Renaissance attempt at a realistic, nonreligious, three-dimensional scene.

Wilton Diptych—scrawny medieval figures Uccello creates a 3-D grid.

Uccello creates the illusion of distance with a background of farmyards, receding hedges, and tiny soldiers. He actually constructs a grid of fallen lances in the foreground, and then places the horses and warriors within it. Still, Uccello hasn't quite worked out the bugs—the figures in the distance are far too big, and the fallen soldier on the left isn't much larger than the fallen shield on the right.

▶ *In Room 56, you'll find a famous Netherlandish masterpiece.*

❸ Van Eyck—*The Arnolfini Portrait* (1434)

Called by some "The Shotgun Wedding," this painting was once thought to depict a wedding ceremony forced by the lady's swelling belly. Today it's understood as a portrait of a solemn, well-dressed, well-heeled couple, the Arnolfinis of Bruges, Belgium. It is a masterpiece of down-to-earth details.

Feel the texture of the fabrics, count the terrier's hairs, trace the shadows generated by the window. Each object is shown in close-up focus; the beads on the back wall are as crystal clear as the bracelets on the woman. To top it off, the round mirror on the far wall reflects the whole scene backward in miniature, showing the loving couple and a pair of mysterious visitors. Is one of them Van Eyck himself at his easel? Or has the artist painted you, the home viewer, into the scene?

By the way, the woman may not be pregnant. The fashion of the day was to wear a pillow to look pregnant in hopes she'd soon get that way. At least, that's what they told their parents.

▶ *Return to Room 55, turn left into Room 57, and enter the...*

Italian Renaissance (Late 1400s)

The Renaissance—or "rebirth" of the culture of ancient Greece and Rome— was a cultural boom that changed people's thinking about every aspect of life. In politics, it meant democracy. In religion, it meant a move away from Church dominance and toward the assertion of man (humanism) and a more personal faith. Science and secular learning were revived after centuries of superstition and ignorance. In architecture, it was a return to the balanced columns and domes of Greece and Rome.

In painting, the Renaissance meant realism. Artists rediscovered the beauty of nature and the human body. With pictures of beautiful people in harmonious, 3-D surroundings, they expressed the optimism and confidence of this new age.

The Arnolfini Portrait—Flemish artists meticulously captured everyday events. Details, details.

❹ Leonardo da Vinci—*The Virgin of the Rocks* (c. 1491-1508)

Mary, the mother of Jesus, plays with her son and little Johnny the Baptist (with cross, at left) while an androgynous angel looks on. Leonardo brings this holy scene right down to earth by setting it among rocks, stalactites, water, and flowering plants. But looking closer, we see that Leonardo has deliberately posed his people into a pyramid shape, with Mary's head at the peak, creating an oasis of maternal stability and serenity amid the hard rock of the earth. Leonardo, who was born illegitimate, may have sought in his art the young mother he never knew. Freud thought so.

▶ *In Room 58, you'll find...*

❺ Botticelli—*Venus and Mars* (c. 1485)

Mars takes a break from war, succumbing to the delights of love (Venus), while impish satyrs play innocently with the discarded tools of death. In the early spring of the Renaissance, there was an optimistic mood in the air—the feeling that enlightened Man could solve all problems. Here, Venus has sapped man's medieval stiffness; the Renaissance has arrived.

▶ *Continue to Room 59.*

❻ Crivelli—*The Annunciation, with Saint Emidius* (1486)

Mary, in green, is visited by the dove of the Holy Spirit, who beams down from the distant heavens in a shaft of light. It's a brilliant collection of realistic details: the hanging rug, the peacock, the architectural minutiae that lead you way, way back, then bam!—you have a giant pickle in your face.

All this is set within Italian Renaissance 3-D. The floor tiles and building bricks recede into the distance. We're sucked right in, accelerating through the alleyway, under the arch, and off into space. The Holy Spirit spans the

Leonardo's *Virgin*—a maternal pyramid

Botticelli revives ancient Greek symbols.

Crivelli's illusion requires no 3-D glasses.

Leonardo's sketch—all eyes lead to Jesus

entire distance, connecting heavenly background with earthly foreground. Crivelli creates an Escheresque labyrinth of rooms and walkways that we want to walk through, around, and into—or is that just a male thing?

Renaissance Italians were interested in—even obsessed with—portraying 3-D space. Perhaps they focused their spiritual passion away from heaven and toward the physical world. With such restless energy, they needed lots of elbow room. Space, the final frontier.

▶ *Continue into Room 60, then turn right into Room 51, where we first entered. In an adjoining room, find a chalk drawing labeled* The Leonardo Cartoon, *and enter the...*

High Renaissance (1490s-Early 1500s)

The "Big Three" of the High Renaissance—Leonardo (whom we saw earlier), Michelangelo, and Raphael—were all Florence-trained. Like Renaissance architects (which they also were), they carefully composed their figures on canvas, "building" them into geometrical patterns that reflected the balance and order they saw in nature.

❼ Leonardo da Vinci—*Virgin and Child with St. Anne and St. John the Baptist* (c. 1499-1500)

This chalk drawing, or cartoon, shows two children at play—oblivious to the violent deaths they'll both suffer—beneath their mothers' Mona Lisa smiles.

But follow the eyes: Shadowy-eyed Anne turns toward Mary, who looks tenderly down to Jesus, who blesses John, who gazes back dreamily. As your eyes follow theirs, you're led back to the literal and psychological center of the composition—Jesus—the Alpha and Omega. This sketch—pieced together from two separate papers (see the line down the middle)—gives us an inside peek at Leonardo's genius.

▶ *From Room 51, cross to the main building (the West Wing) and enter the large Room 9, filled with big colorful canvases from Venice. Turn right and exit at the far end into Room 8.*

❽ Michelangelo, *The Entombment* (c. 1500-1501)

Michelangelo, the greatest sculptor ever, proves it here in this "painted sculpture" of the crucified Jesus being carried to the tomb. Like a chiseled Greek god, this musclehead in red ripples beneath his clothes. Christ's naked body, shocking to the medieval Church, was completely acceptable in the Renaissance world, where classical nudes were admired as an expression of the divine. Regardless of the lack of detail, Michelangelo lets the bodies do the talking.

Renaissance balance and symmetry reign. Christ is the center of the composition, flanked by two people leaning equally, who support his body with strips of cloth. They, in turn, are flanked by two others. The painting is not damaged, but it is unfinished. Michelangelo, 25 years old at the time, moved on to other projects before he got around to adding crucial details, even leaving a blank space in the lower right where Mary would have been.

❾ Raphael, *Pope Julius II* (1511)

The worldly, Renaissance Pope Julius II—who was more a swaggering conquistador than a pious pope—set out to rebuild Rome in Renaissance style, hiring Michelangelo to paint the ceiling of the Vatican's Sistine Chapel.

Raphael gives a behind-the-scenes look at this complex leader. On the one hand, the pope is an imposing pyramid of power, with a velvet

Michelangelo's bodybuilder saints

Raphael—psychological realism

shawl, silk shirt, and fancy rings boasting of wealth and success. But at the same time, he appears bent and broken, his throne backed into a corner, with an expression that seems to say, "Is this all there is?"

▶ *And now for something completely different, still in Room 8.*

MANNERISM (1520s-1600)
Mannerism, developed in reaction to the High Renaissance, subverts the balanced, harmonious ideal of the previous era with exaggerated proportions, asymmetrical compositions, and decorative color.

⑩ Bronzino, *An Allegory with Venus and Cupid* (c.1545)
The right foot of the figure of boy Cupid (standing on the left) was used in the old TV comedy show *Monty Python's Flying Circus*. As the show opened and circus music played, Cupid's giant foot would come down from above to squash the scene with a flatulent *ffft!*

▶ *From Room 8, pass through Room 7 and enter Room 6 for...*

⑪ Tintoretto, *The Origin of the Milky Way* (c. 1575)
The promiscuous god Jupiter places his illegitimate son, baby Hercules, at his wife's breast. Juno says, "Wait a minute. That's not my baby!" Her milk spurts upward, becoming the Milky Way.

Tintoretto places us right up in the clouds, among the gods, who swirl around at every angle. Jupiter appears to be flying almost right at us. An X composition unites it all—Juno slants one way while Jupiter tilts the other.

▶ *Backtrack into the big Room 9. Exit this room at the far end and turn right, entering the long Room 29 (with forest-green wallpaper). Midway through Room 29, turn left and find Room 25.*

Bronzino—Detail of Venus and Cupid feeling frisky   Tintoretto—"That's not my baby!"

Northern Protestant Art (1600s)

We switch from CinemaScope to a tiny TV—smaller canvases, subdued colors, everyday scenes, and not even a bare shoulder.

Money shapes art. The Northern countries' art-buyers were hard-working, middle-class, Protestant merchants. They wanted simple, cheap, no-nonsense pictures to decorate their homes and offices. Greek gods and Virgin Marys were out, hometown folks and hometown places were in—portraits, landscapes, still lifes, and slice-of-life scenes. Painted with great attention to detail, this is art meant not to wow or preach at you, but to be enjoyed and lingered over. Sightsee.

⑫ Vermeer—*A Young Woman Standing at a Virginal* (c. 1670)

Inside a simple but wealthy Dutch home, a prim virgin plays an early piano called a "virginal." We've surprised her, and she pauses to look up at us.

By framing off such a small world to look at—from the blue chair in the foreground to the wall in back—Vermeer forces us to appreciate the tiniest details, the beauty of everyday things. We can meditate on the tiles lining the floor, the subtle shades of the white wall, and the pale, diffused light that seeps in from the window. The painting of a nude cupid on the back wall only strengthens this virgin's purity.

▶ *Also in Room 25, you'll find...*

⑬ Van Hoogstraten, *A Peepshow with Views of the Interior of a Dutch House* (c. 1655-1660)

Look through the open end of this ingenious device to make the painting of a house interior come to three-dimensional life. Compare the twisted curves of the painting with the illusion it creates and appreciate the pains-taking work of the dedicated artist. Painted on the top of the box is another anamorphic projection.

▶ *Enter the adjoining Room 24.*

⑭ Rembrandt—*Belshazzar's Feast* (c. 1635)

The wicked king has been feasting with God's sacred dinnerware when the meal is interrupted. Belshazzar turns to see the hand of God, burning an ominous message into the wall that Belshazzar's number is up. As he turns, he knocks over a goblet of wine. The drama is accentuated by the strong contrast between dark brown and harsh light, a Rembrandt specialty.

Rembrandt captures the scene at the most ironic moment. Belshazzar

Vermeer—the beauty of everyday things

is about to be ruined. We know it, his guests know it, and, judging by the look on his face, he's coming to the same conclusion.

▶ *Nearby (either in Room 24 or in the adjoining Room 23), you'll find...*

⓯ Rembrandt—*Self-Portrait at the Age of 63* (1669)
Rembrandt throws the light of truth on...himself. This craggy self-portrait was done the year he died, at age 63. Contrast it with one done three

Rembrandt—Belshazzar's uh-oh moment

decades earlier (hanging in the previous room). Rembrandt, the greatest Dutch painter, started out as the successful, wealthy young genius of the art world. But he refused to crank out commercial works. Rembrandt painted things that he believed in but no one would invest in—family members, down-to-earth Bible scenes, and self-portraits like these.

Here, Rembrandt surveys the wreckage of his independent life. He was bankrupt, his mistress had just died, and he had also buried several of his children. We see a disillusioned, well-worn, but proud old genius.

▶ *Backtrack to the long, forest-green Room 29.*

Baroque (1600s)

This room holds big, colorful, emotional works by Peter Paul Rubens and others from Catholic Flanders (Belgium). While artists in Protestant and democratic Europe painted simple scenes, those in Catholic and aristocratic countries turned to the style called Baroque. Baroque art took what

Rembrandt—proud self-portrait

Rubens—dimpled-cheek Baroque excess

was flashy in Venetian art and made it flashier, what was gaudy and made it gaudier, what was dramatic and made it shocking.

⑯ Rubens—*The Judgment of Paris* (c. 1636-1639)

Rubens painted anything that would raise your pulse—battles, miracles, hunts, and, especially, fleshy women with dimples on all four cheeks. For instance, *The Judgment of Paris* (one of two versions in this museum by Rubens) is little more than an excuse for a study of the female nude, showing front, back, and profile all on one canvas.

▸ *Exit Room 29 at the far end. In Room 30 (with red wallpaper), on the left-hand wall, you'll find...*

⑰ Velázquez—*The Rokeby Venus* (c. 1647-1651)

Like a Venetian centerfold, Venus lounges diagonally across the canvas, admiring herself, with flaring red, white, and gray fabrics to highlight her rosy-white skin and inflame our passion. Horny Spanish kings loved Titianesque nudes, despite Spain's strict Inquisition. This work by the king's personal court painter is a rare Spanish nude from that ultra-Catholic country. The sole concession to Spanish modesty is the false reflection in the mirror—if it really showed what the angle should show, Velázquez would have needed two mirrors...and a new job.

▸ *From Room 30, turn left into the big, red Room 31, where you'll see a large canvas.*

⑱ Van Dyck—*Equestrian Portrait of Charles I* (c. 1637-1638)

King Charles sits on a huge horse, accentuating his power. The horse's small head makes sure that little Charles isn't dwarfed. Charles was a

Velázquez's racy *Venus*

King Charles I, divine monarch

soft-on-Catholics king in a hard-core Protestant country until England's Civil War (1648), when his genteel head was separated from his refined body by Cromwell and company.

Kings and bishops used the grandiose Baroque style to impress the masses with their power. Van Dyck's portrait style set the tone for all the stuffy, boring portraits of British aristocrats who wished to be portrayed as sophisticated gentlemen—whether they were or not.

▶ *Return to Room 30 and turn left, exiting at the far end, and entering Room 32. On the right wall, find...*

⑲ Caravaggio—*The Supper at Emmaus* (1601)

After Jesus was crucified, he rose from the dead and appeared without warning to some of his followers. Jesus just wants a quiet meal, but the man in green, suddenly realizing who he's eating with, is about to jump out of his chair in shock.

Caravaggio exaggerated the grittiness of life, modeling his saints after real, ugly, unhaloed people. His paintings look like how a wet dog smells. From the torn shirts to the five o'clock shadows, we are witnessing a very human miracle.

▶ *Leave Room 32 at the far end, and enter Room 33.*

French Rococo (1700s)

As Europe's political and economic center shifted from Italy to France, Louis XIV's court at Versailles became its cultural hub. Every aristocrat spoke French, dressed French, and bought French paintings. The Rococo art of Louis' successors was as frilly, sensual, and suggestive as the decadent French court. We see their rosy-cheeked portraits and their fantasies:

Caravaggio—Saints as everyday people

Boucher—Pan seeks a threesome

lords and ladies at play in classical gardens, where mortals and gods cavort together.

▶ *One of the finest examples is the tiny...*

⑳ Boucher—*Pan and Syrinx* (1759)

Curious Pan seeks a threesome, but Syrinx eventually changes to reeds, leaving him all wet. Rococo art is like a Rubens that got shrunk in the wash—smaller, lighter pastel colors, frillier, and more delicate than the Baroque style. Same dimples, though.

▶ *Enter Room 34. Take a hike around and enjoy the English-country-garden ambience.*

British Romantic Art (Early 1800s)

㉑ Constable—*The Hay Wain* (1821)

The reserved British were more comfortable cavorting with nature than with the lofty gods. John Constable set up his easel out-of-doors, making quick sketches to capture the simple majesty of billowing clouds, billowing trees, and everyday rural life. His rustic style was actually considered shocking in its day, scandalizing art lovers used to the highfalutin, prettified sheen of Baroque and Rococo.

㉒ Turner—*The Fighting Téméraire* (1839)

During the Industrial Revolution, machines began to replace humans, factories belched smoke over Constable's hay cart, and cloud-gazers had to punch the clock. Alas, here a modern steamboat symbolically drags a famous but obsolete sailing battleship off into the sunset to be destroyed.

Turner gives us our first glimpse into the modern art world; his messy, colorful style influenced the Impressionists. Turner takes an ordinary scene (like Constable), captures the play of light with messy paints (like Impressionists), and charges it with mystery (like, wow).

► *To view more work by Turner, Constable, and other British artists, visit London's Tate Britain. For now, enter Room 41.*

Impressionism and Beyond (1850-1910)

For 500 years, a great artist was someone who could paint the real world with perfect accuracy. Then along came the camera and, click, the artist was replaced by a machine. But unemployed artists refused to go the way of *The Fighting Téméraire*.

They couldn't match the camera for painstaking detail, but they could match it—even beat it—in capturing color, the fleeting moment, the candid pose, the play of light and shadow, the quick impression a scene makes on you. A new breed of artists bursts out of the stuffy confines of the studio. They donned scarves and berets and set up their canvases in farmers' fields or carried their notebooks into crowded cafés, dashing off quick sketches in order to catch a momentary…impression.

Seurat—lots of dots to "build" a scene

▶ *The Impressionist paintings are scattered throughout Rooms 41-46. Here are a few of my favorites. Start with the misty Monet train station.*

㉓ Monet—*Gare St. Lazare* (1877) and ㉔ *The Water-Lily Pond* (1899)

Claude Monet, the father of Impressionism, was more interested in the play of light off his subject than the subject itself. In *Gare St. Lazare,* he uses smudges of white and gray paint to capture how sun filters through the glass roof of the train station and is refiltered through the clouds of steam.

At his home at Giverny, near Paris, Monet created his own perfect landscape. He planned an artificial garden, rechanneled a stream, built a bridge, and planted water lilies. He painted these scenes time and again, but—because it was always a different day, with different sunlight, inspiring a different mood—each painting was unique.

㉕ Manet—*Corner of a Café-Concert* (1878-1880)

Imagine just how mundane (and therefore shocking) Manet's quick "impression" of this café must have been to a public that was raised on Greek gods, luscious nudes, and glowing Madonnas.

㉖ Seurat—*Bathers at Asnières* (1884)

Viewed from about 15 feet away, this is a bright, sunny scene of people lounging on a riverbank. Now move in close. The "scene" breaks up into almost random patches of bright colors. The "green" grass is a shag rug of green, yellow, red, brown, purple, and white brushstrokes. The boy's "red" cap is a collage of red, yellow, and blue.

▶ *In Room 42, you'll find...*

㉗ Renoir, *The Skiff* (1875)

Move in close. The "scene" breaks up into almost random patches of bright colors. The "blue" water is actually separate brushstrokes of blue, green, pink, purple, gray, and white. The rower's hat is a blob of green, white, and blue. But when you back up to a proper distance, *voilà!* It shimmers. This kind of rough, coarse brushwork is one of the telltale signs of Impressionism. Renoir was not trying to paint the water itself, but the reflection of sky, shore, and boats off its surface.

▶ *In Room 45, you'll see...*

Renoir, *The Skiff*

㉘ Van Gogh—*Sunflowers* (1888)

In military terms, Van Gogh was the point man of his culture. He went ahead of his cohorts, explored the unknown, and caught a bullet young. He added emotion to Impressionism, infusing his love of life even into inanimate objects. These sunflowers, painted with characteristic swirling brushstrokes, shimmer and writhe in either agony or ecstasy—depending on your own mood.

Van Gogh painted these during his stay in southern France, a time of frenzied creativity, when he hovered between agony and ecstasy, bliss and madness. A year later, he shot himself.

In his day, Van Gogh was a penniless nobody, selling only one painting in his whole career. In 1987, a different *Sunflowers* painting (he did a half-dozen versions) sold for $40 million (a salary of about $2,500 a day for 45 years), and that's not even his highest-priced painting. Hmm.

Van Gogh's *Sunflowers* bloom eternally at the National Gallery.

Cézanne bridges Impressionism and Cubism…and brings us into the modern world.

㉙ Cézanne—*Bathers* (c. 1894-1905)

These bathers are arranged in strict triangles à la Leonardo—the five nudes on the left form one triangle, the seated nude on the right forms another, and even the background trees and clouds are triangular patterns of paint.

Cézanne uses the Impressionist technique of building a figure with dabs of paint. But his "dabs" are often larger-sized "cube" shapes that inspired a radical new art style—Cubism.

We've traveled from medieval spirituality to Renaissance realism to Baroque elegance to Impressionist colors. Cézanne brings art into the 20th century. Now complete your walk through history by spilling out into the hubbub of 21st-century London.

▶ *Exiting Room 45, you find yourself in the stairwell of the Gallery's main entrance (under the dome) on Trafalgar Square. If you want to return to the Sainsbury Entrance, cross the stairwell and pass through several rooms (eventually you'll see Michelangelo, Raphael, etc.). When you reach Room 9, turn left to reach the Sainsbury Wing. After perusing 700 years of art—from gold-backed Madonnas to Cubistic bathers—you've earned a well-deserved break.*

West End Walk

From Leicester Square to Piccadilly Circus

The West End, the area just west of the original walled City of London, is London's liveliest neighborhood. Here is where you'll feel the pulse of the living, breathing London of today. Theaters, pubs, restaurants, bookstores, ethnic food, markets, and boutiques attract rock stars, punks, tourists, and ladies and gentlemen stepping from black cabs for a night on the town.

This two-hour walk samples the entertainment energy at Leicester Square, the festivity of Covent Garden, the rock-and-roll history of Denmark Street, the bohemian vibe of Soho, the shopping hustle and bustle of Carnaby and Regent Streets, and the neon hub of Piccadilly Circus.

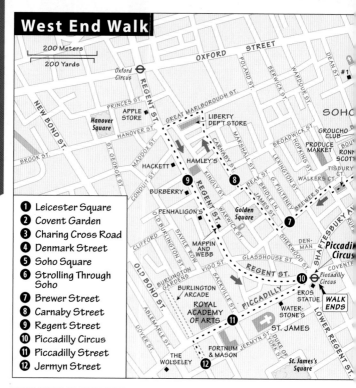

West End Walk

200 Meters
200 Yards

Oxford Circus

OXFORD STREET

POLAND ST.

BERWICK ST.

WARDOUR ST.

DEAN ST.

#1

PRINCES ST.

REGENT ST.

GREAT MARLBOROUGH ST.

LIBERTY DEP'T STORE

SOHO

NEW BOND ST.

APPLE STORE

Hanover Square

HANOVER ST.

BROADWICK ST.

HOPKINS ST.

GROUCHO CLUB

PRODUCE MARKET

RONN SCOTT

ST. GEORGE ST.

BROOK ST.

MADDOX ST.

HACKETT

CONDUIT ST.

HAMLEY'S

❾

CARNABY ST.

MARSHALL ST.

KINGLY ST.

❽

LEXINGTON ST.

BEAK ST.

G. PULTENEY ST.

JAMES ST.

WALKERS CT.

TISBURY CT.

BREWER ST.

BURBERRY

PENHALIGON'S

OLD BURLINGTON ST.

SAVILE ROW

REGENT ST.

WARWICK ST.

Golden Square

SHAFTESBURY AV

❼

CLIFFORD ST.

MAPPIN AND WEBB

GLASSHOUSE ST.

SHERWOOD ST.

DENMAN ST.

Piccadill

Circus

OLD BOND ST.

BURLINGTON GARDENS

VIGO ST.

REGENT ST.

SACKVILLE ST.

Piccadilly Circus

COVENT

ABLEMARLE ST.

BURLINGTON ARCADE

ROYAL ACADEMY OF ARTS

❶❶

PICCADILLY

❶⓪

EROS STATUE

WALK ENDS

LOWER REGENT ST.

DOVER ST.

WATER-STONE'S

ST. JAMES

THE WOLSELEY

FORTNUM & MASON

❶②

JERMYN ST.

DUKE OF YORK ST.

St. James's Square

❶ Leicester Square
❷ Covent Garden
❸ Charing Cross Road
❹ Denmark Street
❺ Soho Square
❻ Strolling Through Soho
❼ Brewer Street
❽ Carnaby Street
❾ Regent Street
❶⓪ Piccadilly Circus
❶❶ Piccadilly Street
❶② Jermyn Street

THE WALK BEGINS

Start at Leicester Square (Tube: Leicester Square). This walk is fun by day (for shopping) or by night (for nightlife). Early evenings are ideal, since most shops stay open at least until 18:00, and there's the bustle of the after-work crowd grabbing dinner or a show.

▶ *Stand at the top of Leicester Square and take in the scene.*

❶ Leicester Square

Leicester (LESS-ter) Square is ground zero for London entertainment. It's

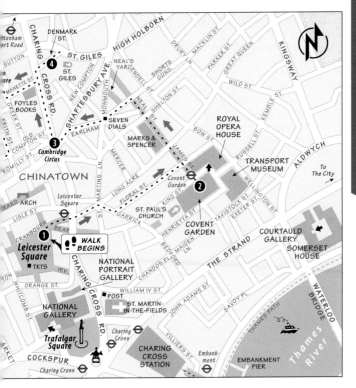

ringed with the city's glitziest **cinemas**—the Odeon (Britain's largest cinema), Empire, and Vue—all famous for hosting red-carpet movie premieres. When Bradley Cooper, Benedict Cumberbatch, Keira Knightley, and Jennifer Lawrence need a publicity splash, it'll likely be here. (Google "London film premieres" to find upcoming events.) On any given night, this entire area is a mosh-pit of club-goers and partying teens in town from the suburbs.

The Square is the central clearinghouse for theater ticket sales. Check out the **tkts kiosk** and ignore all the other establishments that bill themselves as "half-price" (they're just normal booking agencies). It's usually cheaper still to buy tickets directly from one of the theaters we'll pass on this walk.

Capital Radio London (next to the Odeon) plays a role in British rock-and-roll history. Back in the 1960s, the BBC was the only radio station in town, and it was mostly talk and Bach, with a smattering of pop. The British Invasion was in full swing—the Beatles, the Stones, the Who—but Brits couldn't hear it! They had to resort to "pirate" radio stations, beamed from Luxembourg or from ships at sea. Finally in 1973, Capital Radio was allowed to play rock music. Today, FM 95.8 carries on as a major top-40 broadcasting power.

▸ *Exit Leicester Square from its top corner, heading east (past the Vue cinema) on Cranbourn Street. Cross Charing Cross Road and continue along Cranbourn to the six-way intersection, then angle right onto Garrick Street. Shortly afterward, turn left onto calm, brick-lined Floral Street, with its tidy assortment of fashion boutiques. At James Street, turn right and head for...*

❷ Covent Garden

Covent Garden (only tourists pluralize the name) is a large square teeming with people and street performers—jugglers, sword swallowers, and guitar players. London's buskers (including those in the Tube) are auditioned, licensed, and assigned times and places where they are allowed to perform.

The square's centerpiece is an iron-and-glass covered marketplace. A market has been here since medieval times, when it was the "convent" garden owned by Westminster Abbey. Covent Garden remained a

Leicester Square hosts red-carpet premieres.

Covent Garden—browsing the shops

produce market until 1973, when its venerable arcades were converted to boutiques, cafés, and antiques shops. Besides the shops inside, a less formal market scene still thrives around the fringes.

Pan the square to find the world-class **Royal Opera House** (with a low-profile entrance in the northeast corner of the square) and the **London Transport Museum** (southeast corner). **St. Paul's Church** (not the famous cathedral) is to the west, with its Greek temple-like facade and blue clock face. St. Paul's is known as the Actors' Church, and its interior is lined with memorials to theater folk, some of whom (Chaplin, Karloff) you might recognize. The church is still a favorite of nervous performers praying for success.

▶ *Now browse your way northwest, along some lively and colorful streets.*

❸ From Covent Garden to Charing Cross Road

First backtrack two blocks up James Street, then continue straight (along the side of Marks & Spencer department store) up narrow Neal Street. Turn left on Short's Gardens, and find the tight alley (on the right) leading to the cozy, funky courtyard called Neal's Yard, with a thriving veggie restaurant scene. Back on Short's Gardens, Neal's Yard Dairy (at #17) sells a wide variety of artisanal cheeses from the British Isles, and gives out samples if you ask nicely.

Continue along Short's Gardens to the next intersection—called **Seven Dials**—where seven sundials atop a pole mark the meeting of seven small streets. Continue more or less straight ahead onto Earlham Street.

Bearing left, you'll spill out into **Cambridge Circus**—the busy intersection of Shaftesbury Avenue and Charing Cross Road—with its fine red-brick Victorian architecture and classic theaters. **Charing Cross Road** is the traditional home of London's bookstores.

▶ *Turn right (north) up Charing Cross Road. You'll pass one of the biggest bookstores, Foyles Books, which often hosts free book signings and jazz music (usually around 18:00, at 107 Charing Cross Road, www. foyles.co.uk).*

Continue a few steps north on Charing Cross, and turn right onto Denmark Street.

Seven Dials intersection

Denmark Street—home of British rock and roll

❹ Denmark Street

This seemingly nondescript little street is a musician's mecca. In the 1920s, it was known as "Britain's Tin Pan Alley"—the center of the UK's music-publishing industry, when songwriters here cranked out popular tunes printed as sheet music.

Later, in the 1960s, Denmark Street was the epicenter of rock and roll's British Invasion, which brought so much great pop music to the US. **Regent Sound Studio** (at #4, on the right) was a low-budget recording studio. It was one of several studios on the street that recorded the Rolling Stones ("Not Fade Away"), the Kinks ("Denmark Street"), the Beatles ("Fixing a Hole"), and the Who ("Happy Jack"). Today, Regent is a music store.

The storefront at #20 (on the left, now Wunjo Guitars) was formerly a music publishing house, which employed a lowly office boy named Reginald Dwight. In 1969, on the building's rooftop, he wrote "Your Song," and went on to become famous as Sir Elton John. In the 1970s, the Sex Pistols lived in apartments above #6 (on the right). The 12 Bar Café at #25, on the left (now closed), helped launch the careers of more recent acts: Damien Rice, KT Tunstall, Jeff Buckley, and Keane.

Today, Denmark Street offers one-stop shopping for the modern musician. Without leaving this short street, you could buy a vintage Rickenbacker guitar, get your sax repaired, take piano lessons, lay down a bass track, have a few beers, or tattoo your name across your knuckles like Ozzy Osbourne. Notice the bulletin board in the alley alongside the 12 Bar Café (through the doorway marked #27). If you're a musician looking for a band to play in, this could be your connection.

▶ *From Denmark Street, go back across Charing Cross Road and head down Manette Street (alongside Foyles). Pass by the Borderline nightclub (down the lane called Orange Yard), where R.E.M. and Oasis have played. Continue down Manette Street and under the passage, then turn right up Greek Street to...*

❺ Soho Square

The Soho neighborhood is London's version of New York City's Greenwich Village. It's ritzy, raffish, edgy, and colorful. Having escaped modern urban development, it retains a quiet, residential, pedestrian-friendly feel.

Soho Square Gardens is a favorite place on a sunny afternoon. The little house in the middle of the square is the gardener's hut. At #1, on the west (left) side of the square, the MPL building (McCartney Publishing Limited) houses offices of Britain's richest musician, Sir Paul McCartney.

▶ *At the bottom of the square, wander down Frith Street.*

❻ Strolling Through Soho

The restaurants and boutiques here and on adjoining streets (e.g., Greek, Dean, and Wardour streets) are trendy and creative, the kind that attract high society when they feel like slumming it. Bars with burly, well-dressed bouncers abound.

Ronnie Scott's Jazz Club (at #47 Frith Street) has featured big-name acts for 50-plus years. In 1970, Jimi Hendrix jammed here with Eric Burdon and War in the last performance before his death, a few days later, in a London apartment.

Turn right on Old Compton Street. You're at the center of the neighborhood (and London's gay scene), surrounded by the buzz of Soho. Take in the eclectic variety of people going by.

At the corner of Old Compton and Dean Street, look left on Dean Street. The pagoda-style arch in the distance marks London's underwhelming Chinatown, with Gerrard Street as its spine.

▶ *Continue along Old Compton Street to where it squeezes down into a narrow alley (Tisbury Court). Penetrate this sleazy passage of sex shows and blue-video shops, tolerate the barkers' raunchy come-ons, then jog a half-block right and turn left on Brewer Street.*

❼ Brewer Street: Sleaze, Porn Shops, and Prostitutes

Soho was a bordello zone in the 19th century. A bit of that survives today in this area. Sex shops, video arcades, and prostitution mingle with upscale restaurants here in west Soho. While it's illegal in Britain to sell sex on

Soho's Chinatown—less inviting than it looks   Soho—still some seediness amid the glitz

the street, well-advertised "models" entertain (profitably) in their tiny apartments. Berwick Street hosts a daily produce market.

▶ *When you reach the intersection of Brewer Street and Sherwood Street (which is also called Lower James Street), turn right and walk two blocks north (on what is now called Upper James Street). Then jog left at Beak Street to find...*

❽ Carnaby Street

In the Swinging '60s, when Pete Townshend needed a paisley shirt, John Lennon a Nehru jacket, or Twiggy a miniskirt, they came here—where those mod fashions were invented. Today, there's not a hint of hippie. For the most part, Carnaby Street looks like everything else from the '60s does now—sanitized and co-opted by upscale franchises. At least the upper end of the street retains a whiff of funkiness.

▶ *Walk north, the length of Carnaby Street, turn left on Great Marlborough Street, and head to Regent Street. You'll pass the venerable Liberty department store in the faux-Tudor building, known for its "Liberty Print" patterned cloth. At Regent Street, begin strolling downhill.*

❾ The Shops of Regent Street

You're in the heart of London's high-class, top-dollar shopping neighborhood. Regent Street has wide sidewalks and fine architecture, and most of the shops call the Queen their landlord, as she owns much of the land.

Just downhill from Liberty, follow the giddy kids to **Hamleys** (at #188-196), Britain's biggest toy store. It's been delighting children for more than 250 years. It was here that the world first got to know the Build-a-Bear workshop (now a fixture at malls everywhere) and Britain's genteel

Paddington Bear. Seven floors buzz with 28,000 toys, managed by a staff of 200. Employees, some dressed in playful costumes, give demos of the latest gadgets.

Continuing along the street, you'll pass fine bits of old English class. **Hackett** (across from Hamleys at #193) is the place to go for preppy young English menswear. **Mappin and Webb** (left, at #132) is the queen's jeweler. **Penhaligon's** (right, at #125) is the quintessential English perfumery, where royals shop for classic English scents like lavender and rose. Once dowdy—it's a clothier of the royal family—**Burberry** (on the right, at #121) is now hip.

▶ *Regent Street arcs seductively into the ever-vibrant...*

⑩ Piccadilly Circus

London's most touristy square got its name from the fancy ruffled

Regent Street bends with the latest fashion trends.

Piccadilly—Eros statue and neon ads

Beau Brummel welcomes gentlemen shoppers.

shirts—**picadils**—made in the neighborhood long ago. In the late 20th century, the square veered toward the gimmicky and tacky—look no further than the gargantuan Ripley's Believe-It-or-Not Museum.

But recently, it's become more pedestrian-friendly and trendy. The tipsy-but-perfectly-balanced Eros statue marks the center of this people magnet. Kitschy stores like **Lillywhites** and **Cool Brittania** dispense English soccer jerseys and Union Jack underwear. At night, when neon pulses, the 20-foot-high video ads paint the classic Georgian facades in a rainbow of colors. Black cabs honk, tourists crowd the attractions, and Piccadilly shows off big-city London at its glitziest.

▶ *Your walk is over. If you have more energy, you could head west down* ⓫ *Piccadilly Street to the Fortnum & Mason department store (#181), with its classy ambience and traditional afternoon tea. A half-block farther along Piccadilly Street, a left turn down the Piccadilly Arcade leads to quiet* ⓬ *Jermyn Street. A statue of Beau Brummell, the ultimate dandy, welcomes you to this neighborhood of clothing stores that have catered to upper-class gentlemen for generations. Pick up an elegant ascot or bowler hat, or head back to Piccadilly Square.*

British Museum Tour

In the 19th century, the British flag flew over one-fourth of the world, and England collected art as fast as it collected colonies. The British Museum became the chronicle of Western civilization. It's the only place I can think of where you can follow the rise and fall of three great cultures in a few hours with a coffee break in the middle.

See pharaohs and their mummies from ancient Egypt, and the multilingual Rosetta Stone. From mighty Assyria come truck-sized statues and poignant scenes of hunted lions. The finale is the Elgin Marbles, the renowned sculptures that once decorated the Parthenon of Golden Age Greece. While the sun never set on the British Empire, it will set on you, so on this tour we'll see just the most exciting two hours.

ORIENTATION

Cost: Free, but a £5 donation is suggested. Interesting temporary exhibits often require a separate admission.

Hours: Open daily 10:00-17:30, Fri until 20:30 (not all galleries).

Avoiding Crowds: Rainy days and Sundays are most crowded; weekday late afternoons, especially on Fridays, are least crowded.

Getting There: The main entrance is on Great Russell Street. From the Tottenham Court Road Tube station, take exit #3, turn right, and follow the brown signs four blocks to the museum. The Holborn and Russell Square Tube stops are also nearby.

Information: General info tel. 020/7323-8299, www.britishmuseum.org. For questions on the collection, call 020/7323-8838.

Tours: Free 30- to 40-minute EyeOpener tours focus on select rooms (offered about every 15 minutes). The £5 multimedia guide offers dial-up info on 200 objects, as well as several theme tours. You can 🎧 download this chapter as a free Rick Steves audio tour (✪ see page 201).

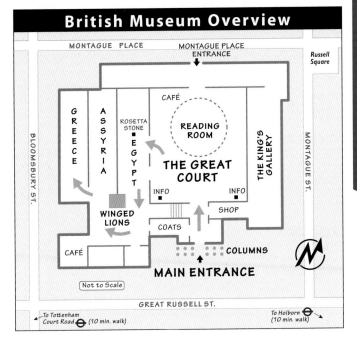

Cloakroom: £1.50 per item. Large backpacks must be checked.

Photography: Photos allowed without flash or tripod (but prohibited in the temporary exhibits).

Cuisine Art: In the Great Court entrance lobby, there's the self-service $ Court Café on ground level (sandwiches and salads) and the pricier $$$ Court Restaurant up the stairs (entrees). The cafeteria-style $$ Gallery Café (offers hot dishes) is deeper into the museum, near the Greek art in Room 12. Near the museum, there are lots of fast, cheap, and colorful eateries along Great Russell Street.

Starring: The Rosetta Stone, Egyptian mummies, Assyrian lions, and the Parthenon sculptures.

THE TOUR BEGINS

The main entrance on Great Russell Street spills you into the Great Court, a glass-domed space with the round Reading Room in the center. (The Reading Room is impressive to visit, but not always open to visitors.) From the Great Court, doorways lead to all wings. To the left—in the West Wing—are the exhibits on Egypt, Assyria, and Greece—our tour.

▶ *Enter the Egyptian Gallery. The Rosetta Stone is directly in front of you.*

Ancient Egypt (3000 B.C.-A.D. 1)

Egypt was one of the world's first "civilizations"—that is, a group of people with a government, religion, art, a written language, and the free time to appreciate them. The Egypt we think of—pyramids, mummies, pharaohs, and guys who walk funny—lasted from 3000 to 1000 B.C. with hardly any change in the government, religion, or arts.

❶ The Rosetta Stone (196 B.C.)

When this rock was unearthed in the Egyptian desert in 1799, it was a sensation in Europe. This black slab caused a quantum leap in the evolution of history. Finally, Egyptian writing could be decoded.

The hieroglyphic writing in the upper part of the stone was indecipherable for a thousand years. Did a picture of a bird mean "bird"? Or was it a sound, forming part of a larger word, like "burden"? As it turned out, hieroglyphics are a complex combination of the two, surprisingly more phonetic than symbolic. (For example, the hieroglyph that looks like a mouth or an eye is the letter "R.")

Rosetta Stone—inscribed in three languages

Ramesses II—a truck-sized statue fragment

British Museum–Egypt

ASSYRIA

To ❺ & ❻ & ❼

WINGED
LIONS

❾

❶

❽   ❷   ❹

❸

❶❶ ❶❷

❶❷ ❶❶ ❶❶

C
L
O
A
K
R
O
O
M

Not to Scale

GREAT
COURT &
READING
ROOM

❶ Rosetta Stone

❷ King Ramesses II

❸ Egyptian Gods as Animals

❹ Colossal Scarab

❺ Up to Nebamun Hunting
   in the Marshes

❻ Up to Mummies & Coffins

❼ Gebelein Man

❽ Head & Arm of Amenhotep III

❾ Four Figures of Sekhmet

❿ Beard Piece of Great Sphinx

⓫ False Door & Architrave
   of Ptahshepses

⓬ Statue of Nenkheftka

The Rosetta Stone allowed linguists to break the code. It contains a single inscription repeated in three languages. The bottom third is plain old Greek (find your favorite frat or sorority), while the middle is ancient Egyptian script. By comparing the two known languages with the one they didn't know, translators figured out the hieroglyphics.

The breakthrough came when they discovered that the large ovals (e.g., in the sixth line from the top) represented the name of the ruler, Ptolemy. Simple.

▶ In the gallery to the right of the Stone, find the huge head of Ramesses.

❷ King Ramesses II (c. 1250 B.C.)

When Moses told the king of Egypt, "Let my people go!" this was the stony-faced look he got. Ramesses II ruled for 66 years (c. 1290-1223 B.C.) and may have been in power when Moses (as the Bible says) cursed Egypt

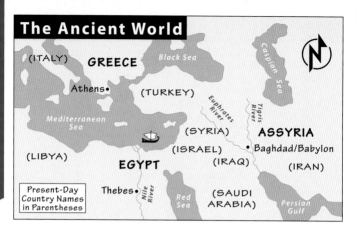

The Ancient World

(ITALY) **GREECE** *Black Sea* *Caspian Sea*

Athens• (TURKEY) *Euphrates River* *Tigris River*

Mediterranean Sea **ASSYRIA**

(SYRIA) • Baghdad/Babylon

(LIBYA) (ISRAEL)

EGYPT (IRAQ) (IRAN)

Present-Day Country Names in Parentheses

Thebes• *Nile River* *Red Sea* (SAUDI ARABIA) *Persian Gulf*

with plagues, freed the Israeli slaves, and led them out of Egypt to their homeland in Israel. This seven-ton statue, made from two different colors of granite, is a fragment from a temple in Thebes. It shows Ramesses with the traditional features of a pharaoh—goatee, cloth headdress, and cobra diadem on his forehead. Ramesses was a great builder of temples, palaces, tombs, and statues of himself. There are probably more statues of him in the world than there are cheesy fake Davids. He was so concerned about achieving immortality that he even chiseled his own name on other people's statues. Very cheeky.

▶ *Climb the ramp behind Ramesses, looking for animals.*

❸ Egyptian Gods as Animals

The Egyptians worshipped animals as incarnations of the gods. The powerful ram is the god Amun (king of the gods), protecting a puny pharaoh under his powerful chin. The falcon is Horus, the god of the living. The speckled, standing hippo (with lion head) is Tawaret—pregnant and grimacing in labor as the protectress of childbirth. Finally, the cat (with ear- and nose-rings) served Bastet, the popular goddess of stress relief.

▶ *At the end of the Egyptian Gallery—past several large stone coffins—is a big stone beetle.*

❹ Colossal Scarab (c. 332 B.C.)

This species of beetle would burrow into the ground, then reappear—it's a symbol of resurrection, like the sun rising and setting, or death and rebirth. Scarab amulets were placed on mummies' chests to protect the spirit's heart from acting impulsively. Pharaohs wore the symbol of the beetle, and tombs and temples were decorated with them. The hieroglyph for scarab meant "to come into being."

▶ *You can't call Egypt a wrap until you visit the mummies upstairs. Continue to the end of the gallery past the giant stone scarab and up the West Stairs (four flights or elevator) to floor 3. Turn left into Room 61, with objects and wall paintings from the tomb of Nebamun.*

❺ Painting of Nebamun Hunting in the Marshes (c. 1350 B.C.)

Nebamun stands in a reed boat, gliding through the marshes. He raises his arm, ready to bean a bird with a snakelike hunting stick.

This nobleman walks like Egyptian statues look—stiff and flat, like he was just run over by a pyramid. We see the torso from the front and everything else—arms, legs, face—in profile, creating the funny walk that has become an Egyptian cliché.

But the stiffness is softened by a human touch. It's a snapshot of a family outing. On the right, his wife looks on, while his daughter crouches between his legs, a symbol of fatherly protection. There's even the family cat (thigh-high, in front of the man) acting as a retriever—possibly the only cat in history that ever did anything useful.

When Nebamun passed into the afterlife, his awakening soul could look at this painting on the tomb wall and think of his loved ones for all eternity.

Scarab—beetle symbolizing rebirth

Nebamun—surprisingly realistic family scene

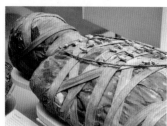

Mummy—preserving bodies for the afterlife   "Ginger"—5,400-year-old corpse

▶ *Browse through Rooms 62-63, filled with displays in glass cases.*

❻ The Egyptian Funeral

To mummify a body: Disembowel it (but leave the heart inside), pack the cavities with pitch, and dry it with natron, a natural form of sodium carbonate (and, I believe, the active ingredient in Twinkies). Then carefully bandage it head to toe with hundreds of yards of linen strips. Let it sit 2,000 years, and...*poof, Bob's your uncle!*

The mummy was placed in a wooden coffin, which was put in a stone coffin, which was placed in a tomb. (The pyramids were supersized tombs for the rich and famous.) The result is that we now have Egyptian bodies that are as well preserved as Larry King.

The internal organs were preserved alongside the mummy in canopic jars, and small-scale statuettes of the deceased *(shabtis)* were scattered around. Written in hieroglyphs on the coffins and the tomb walls were burial rites from the Book of the Dead. These were magical spells to protect the body and crib notes for the waking soul, who needed to know these passwords to get past the guardians of eternity.

Browse these rooms, noticing the Roman-era portraits of the deceased and the mummies of cats (Room 62). Worshiped in life as the sun god's allies, preserved in death, and memorialized with statues, cats were given the adulation they've come to expect ever since.

▶ *In Room 64, in a glass case, you'll find what's left of a visitor who tried to see the entire museum in one visit.*

❼ Gebelein Man, Known as "Ginger"

This man died 5,400 years ago, a thousand years before the pyramids. His people buried him in the fetal position, where he could "sleep" for eternity. The hot sand naturally dehydrated and protected the body. With him are a few of his possessions: bowls, beads, and the flint blade next to his arm. His grave was covered with stones. Named "Ginger" by scientists for his wisps of red hair, this man from a distant time seems very human.

▶ *Backtrack to Room 61 and head back down the stairs to the Egyptian Gallery and the Rosetta Stone. Just past the Rosetta Stone, find a huge head (facing away from you) with a hat like a bowling pin.*

❽ Head and Arm of a Statue of Amenhotep III (c. 1370 B.C.)

Art served as propaganda for the pharaohs, kings who called themselves gods on earth. Put this red granite head on top of an enormous body (which still stands in Egypt), and you have the intimidating image of an omnipotent ruler who demands servile obedience. Next to the head is, appropriately, the pharaoh's powerful fist—the long arm of the law. The crown is actually two crowns in one. The pointed upper half is the royal cap of Upper Egypt. This rests on the flat, fez-like crown symbolizing Lower Egypt. A pharaoh wearing both crowns together is bragging that he rules a combined Egypt.

▶ *Along the wall to the left of the red granite head (as you're facing it) are four black lion-headed statues.*

❾ Four Figures of the Goddess Sekhmet (c. 1360 B.C.)

The lion-headed goddess Sekhmet looks pretty sedate here, but she could spring into a fierce crouch when crossed. She was the pharaoh's

Red Granite Head—fragment of a colossus

Sekhmet—the lion-headed goddess

personal bodyguard, who could burn his enemies to a crisp with flaming arrows. Sekhmet holds an ankh. This key-shaped cross was the hieroglyph meaning "life" and was a symbol of eternal life. Later, it was adopted as a Christian symbol because of its cross shape and religious overtones.

▶ *Continuing down the Egyptian Gallery, a few paces directly in front of you and to the left, find a glass case containing a...*

⑩ Beard Piece of the Great Sphinx

The Great Sphinx—a statue of a pharaoh-headed lion—crouches in the shadow of the Great Pyramids in Cairo. Time shaved off the sphinx's soft, goatee-like limestone beard, and a piece is now preserved here in a glass case. This hunk of stone is only a whisker—about three percent of the massive beard—giving an idea of the scale of the six-story-tall, 250-foot-long statue.

▶ *Ten steps past the Sphinx's soul patch is a 10-foot-tall, red-tinted "building" covered in hieroglyphics.*

⑪ False Door and Architrave of Ptahshepses (c. 2400 B.C.)

This limestone "false door" was a ceremonial entrance (never meant to open) for a sealed building, called a *mastaba,* that marked the grave of a man named Ptahshepses. The hieroglyphs of eyes, birds, and rabbits serve as his epitaph, telling his life story, how he went to school with the pharaoh's kids, became an honored vizier, and married the pharaoh's daughter.

The deceased was mummified, placed in a wooden coffin that was encased in a stone coffin, then in a stone sarcophagus (like the **red-granite sarcophagus** in front of Ptahshepses' door), and buried 50 feet beneath the *mastaba* in an underground chamber.

Mastabas like Ptahshepses' were decorated inside and out with statues, steles, and frescoes like those displayed nearby. These pictured the things that the soul would find useful in the next life—magical spells, lists of the deceased's accomplishments, snapshots of the deceased and his family while alive, and secret passwords from the Egyptian Book of the Dead. False doors like this allowed the soul—but not grave robbers—to come and go.

▶ *Just past Ptahshepses' false door is a glass case with a statue.*

⑫ Statue of Nenkheftka (c. 2400 B.C.)

Originally standing in a "false door" of his *mastaba,* this painted statue

Limestone false door—spirits enter here

Nenkheftka's soul takes a walk.

represented the soul of the deceased. Meant to keep alive the memory and personality of the departed, this image would have greeted Nenkheftka's loved ones when they brought food offerings to place at his feet to nourish his soul. (In the mummification rites, the mouth was ritually opened, to prepare it to eat soul food.)

In ancient Egypt, you *could* take it with you. After you died, your soul lived on, enjoying its earthly possessions—sometimes including servants, who might be walled up alive with their master. (Remember that even the great pyramids were just big tombs for Egypt's most powerful.)

Statues functioned as a refuge for the soul on its journey after death. The rich scattered statues of themselves everywhere, just in case. Statues needed to be simple and easy to recognize, mug shots for eternity: stiff, arms down, chin up, nothing fancy. This one has all the essential features, like the stylized human figures on international traffic signs. To a soul caught in the fast lane of astral travel, this symbolic statue would be easier to spot than a detailed one.

With their fervent hope for life after death, Egyptians created calm, dignified art that seems built for eternity.

▶ *Relax. One civilization down, two to go. Near the end of the gallery, on the right, are two huge, winged Assyrian lions (with bearded human heads) standing guard over the Assyrian exhibit halls.*

Ancient Assyria (900-600 B.C.)

Long before Saddam Hussein, Iraq was home to other palace-building, iron-fisted rulers—the Assyrians.

Assyria was the lion, the king of beasts of early Middle Eastern civilizations. These Semitic people from the agriculturally challenged hills of

British Museum—Assyria

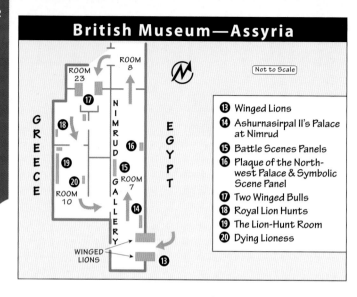

ROOM 23

ROOM 8

Not to Scale

GREECE

NIMRUD GALLERY

EGYPT

ROOM 7

ROOM 10

WINGED LIONS

⑬ Winged Lions
⑭ Ashurnasirpal II's Palace at Nimrud
⑮ Battle Scenes Panels
⑯ Plaque of the North-west Palace & Symbolic Scene Panel
⑰ Two Winged Bulls
⑱ Royal Lion Hunts
⑲ The Lion-Hunt Room
⑳ Dying Lioness

northern Iraq became traders and conquerors, not farmers. They conquered their southern neighbors and dominated the Middle East for 300 years.

Their strength came from a superb army (chariots, mounted cavalry, and siege engines), a policy of terrorism against enemies ("I tied their heads to tree trunks all around the city," reads a royal inscription), ethnic cleansing and mass deportations of the vanquished, and efficient administration (roads and express postal service). They have been called the "Romans of the East."

⑬ Two Human-Headed Winged Lions (c. 11th-8th century B.C.)

These stone lions guarded an Assyrian palace. With the strength of a lion, the wings of an eagle, the brain of a man, and the beard of ZZ Top, they protected the king from evil spirits and scared the heck out of foreign ambassadors and left-wing newspaper reporters. (What has five legs and flies? Take a close look. These quintupeds, which appear complete from both the front and the side, could guard both directions at once.)

Carved into the stone between the bearded lions' loins, you can see

Assyrian winged lions standing guard

Assyrian King—a powerful conqueror

one of civilization's most impressive achievements—writing. This wedge-shaped (cuneiform) script is the world's first written language, invented 5,000 years ago by the Sumerians (of southern Iraq) and passed down to their less-civilized descendants, the Assyrians.

▶ *Walk between the lions, glance at the large reconstructed wooden gates from an Assyrian palace, and turn right into the long, narrow red gallery (Room 7) lined with stone relief panels.*

⓮ Ashurnasirpal II's Palace at Nimrud (9th century B.C.)

This gallery is a mini version of the throne room of King Ashurnasirpal II's palace at Nimrud. Entering, you'd see the king on his throne at the far end, surrounded by these pleasant, sand-colored, gypsum relief panels (which were, however, originally painted and varnished).

That's Ashurnasirpal himself in the **first panel on your right,** with braided beard, earring, fez-like crown, and bulging forearms, flanked by his supernatural hawk-headed henchmen, who sprinkle incense on him with pine cones. Ashurnasirpal II (r. 883-859 B.C.) was a conqueror's conqueror, and the room's panels chronicle his bloody career.

▶ *A dozen paces farther down, on the left wall, are several relief panels (among many in this room) that are worth focusing on.*

⓯ Panels with Battle Scenes

Attack on an Enemy Town: The Assyrians lay siege to a walled city with a crude "tank." It shields them as they smash down the gate with a battering ram. The king stands a safe distance away behind the juggernaut and bravely shoots arrows.

Enemy Escape: Just ahead, **in the lower panel,** enemy soldiers flee the slings and arrows of outrageous Assyrians by swimming across the Euphrates, using inflated animal bladders as life preservers. Their friends in the castle downstream applaud their ingenuity.

Review of Prisoners: After that, prisoners are paraded before the Assyrian king, who is shaded by a parasol. Above the prisoners' heads, we see the spoils of war—elephant tusks, metal pots, etc.—that fueled the Assyrian economy. The Assyrian king sneers and tells the captured chief, "Drop and give me 50."

▸ *On the opposite wall is an artist's rendering of what the palace would have looked like.*

⑯ Plaque of the Northwest Palace and Symbolic Scene Panel

The plaque shows the king at the far end of the throne room, flanked by winged lions. The 30,000-square-foot palace was built atop a 50-acre artificial mound. The new palace was inaugurated with a 10-day banquet, where the king picked up the tab for 69,574 of his closest friends.

The relief panel (immediately to the right) labeled ***Symbolic Scene*** stood behind the throne. It shows the king (and his double) tending the tree of life while reaching up to receive the ring of kingship from the winged sun god.

▸ *Exit the gallery at the far end, then hang a U-turn left. Pause at the entrance of Room 10c to see the impressive...*

⑰ Two Winged Bulls from the Palace of Sargon (c. 710-705 B.C.)

These marble bulls guarded the entrance to a vast palace complex built by Sargon II (r. 721-705 B.C.) near ancient Nineveh and Nimrud (today's Mosul). The 30-ton bulls were cut from a single block, tipped on their sides, and then dragged to their place by POWs. In modern times, when the British transported them here, they had to cut them in half; you can see the horizontal cracks through the bulls' chests.

It was Sargon II who subdued the Israelites after a three-year siege of Jerusalem (2 Kings 17:1-6). He solidified his conquest by ethnically cleansing the area and deporting many Israelites, inspiring legends of the "Lost" Ten Tribes.

▸ *Sneak between these bulls and veer right (into Room 10), where horses are being readied for the big hunt.*

⑱ Royal Lion Hunts from the North Palace of Ashurbanipal

On the right wall are horses; on the left are the hunting dogs. And next to them, lions, resting peacefully in a garden, unaware that they will shortly be rousted, stampeded, and slaughtered.

Lions lived in Mesopotamia up until modern times, and it was the king's duty to keep the lion population down to protect farmers and herdsmen. When this duty became sport, the kings of men proved their power by taking on the king of beasts.

▶ *Continue ahead into the larger lion-hunt room. Reading the panels like a comic strip, start on the right and gallop counterclockwise.*

⑲ The Lion-Hunt Room (c. 650 B.C.)

These panels show Assyria's sport of kings: lion hunting. The king's men release the lions from their cages, then riders on horseback herd them into an enclosed arena. The king (in the chariot) has them cornered. Having left

These two winged bulls once guarded the entrance to Sargon's palace in (what is now) Iraq.

a half-dozen corpses in his wake, he moves on, while spearmen hold off lions attacking from the rear.

▶ *At about the middle of the long wall...*

The fleeing lions, cornered by hounds, shot through with arrows, and weighed down by fatigue, begin to fall. The lead lion carries on even while vomiting blood.

▶ *On the wall opposite the vomiting lion is the...*

⑳ Dying Lioness

A lioness roars in pain and frustration. She tries to run, but her body is too heavy. Her muscular hind legs, once the source of her power, are now paralyzed. Like these brave, fierce lions, Assyria's once-great warrior nation was slain. A generation after these panels were carved, Assyria was conquered, and the capital at Nineveh was sacked and looted (612 B.C.) by the Babylonians from modern Baghdad. The mood of tragedy, dignity, and proud struggle in a hopeless cause makes this dying lioness simply one of the most beautiful of human creations.

Dying lioness—tragic art of a dying civilization

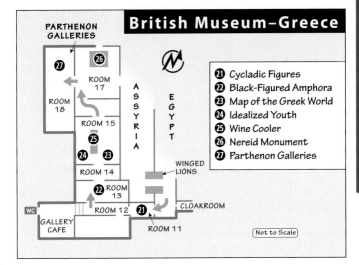

PARTHENON
GALLERIES

British Museum–Greece

ROOM 17
ROOM 18
ROOM 15
ROOM 14
ROOM 13
ROOM 12
ROOM 11
GALLERY CAFÉ
WC
WINGED LIONS
CLOAKROOM
ASSYRIA
EGYPT

㉑ Cycladic Figures
㉒ Black-Figured Amphora
㉓ Map of the Greek World
㉔ Idealized Youth
㉕ Wine Cooler
㉖ Nereid Monument
㉗ Parthenon Galleries

Not to Scale

▶ *Exit the lion-hunt room at the far end and make your way back to the huge, winged lions at the start of the Assyrian exhibit. To reach the Greek section, exit Assyria between the winged lions and make a U-turn to the right, into Room 11.*

You'll walk past ㉑ early Greek Barbie and Ken dolls from the Cycladic period (2500 B.C.). Continue into Room 12 (the hungry can go straight to the Gallery Café), and turn right, into Room 13, filled with Greek vases in glass cases. Pottery, mostly painted red and black, was a popular export product for the sea-trading Greeks.

Ancient Greece (600 B.C.- A.D. 1)
During its Golden Age (500-430 B.C.), Greece set the tone for all of Western civilization to follow. Democracy, theater, literature, mathematics, philosophy, science, gyros, art, and architecture, as we know them, were virtually all invented by a single generation of Greeks in a small town of maybe 80,000 citizens. But Greece wasn't always Golden. The museum traces the evolution of Greek art and culture, from crude and barbaric to sophisticated and civilized.

Achilles exchanges meaningful eye contact.

Wine cooler—Greeks valued balanced art

▶ *Roughly in the middle of Room 13 is a Z-shaped glass case marked #8. On the lower shelf, the item marked #231 is a...*

㉒ Black-Figured Amphora with Achilles Killing Penthesilea (540-530 B.C.)

Greeks poured wine from jars like this one, painted with a man stabbing a woman, a legend from the Trojan War.

On the vessel, Achilles of Greece faces off against the Queen of the Amazons, Penthesilea. Achilles bears down, plunging a spear through her neck, as the blood spurts. In her dying moment, Penthesilea looks up, her gaze locking on Achilles. His eyes bulge wide, and he falls instantly in love with her. She dies, and Achilles is smitten.

▶ *Continue to Room 15. On the entrance wall, find a...*

㉓ Map of the Greek World (520-430 B.C.)

After Greece drove out Persian invaders in 480 B.C., the city of Athens became the most powerful of the city-states and the center of the Greek world. By 300 B.C., the conqueror Alexander the Great had forged a Greek-speaking, "Hellenistic" empire that stretched from Italy and Egypt to India. Two hundred years later, this Greek-speaking world was conquered and assimilated by the Romans.

▶ *There's a nude male statue on the left side of the room.*

㉔ Torso of an Idealized Youth (Kouros, c. 520-510 B.C.)

The Greeks saw their gods in human form...and human beings were god-like. With his perfectly round head, symmetrical pecs, and navel in the center, the youth exemplifies the divine orderliness of the universe. The ideal statue was geometrically perfect, a balance between movement and stillness, between realistic human anatomy (with human flaws) and the perfection of a Greek god. This boy is still a bit uptight, stiff as the rock from which he's carved. But—as we'll see—in just a few short decades, the Greeks would cut loose and create realistic statues that seemed to move like real humans.

▶ *Two-thirds of the way down Room 15 (on the left) is a glass case containing a vase.*

㉕ Red-Figured Wine Cooler Signed by Douris as Painter (490 B.C.)

This clay vessel, called a *psykter,* was designed to float in a bowl of cooling water and shows satyrs at a symposium, or drinking party. These half-man/half-animal creatures (notice their tails) had a reputation for lewd behavior, reminding the balanced and moderate Greeks of their rude roots.

The reveling figures painted on this jar are impressively realistic, three-dimensional, and fluid. The Greeks are beginning to find the balance

Nereid Monument—a mini-Parthenon with similar features: pediment, frieze, and metopes

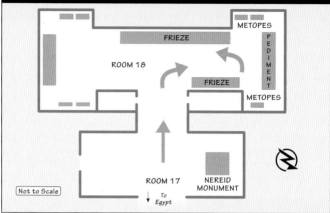

British Museum–Parthenon Galleries

METOPES

FRIEZE

ROOM 18

P E D I M E N T

FRIEZE

METOPES

ROOM 17

NEREID MONUMENT

Not to Scale

↓ To Egypt

between stillness and motion. And speaking of "balance," if that's a Greek sobriety test, revel on.

▸ *Carry on into Room 17 and sit facing the Greek temple at the far end.*

㉖ Nereid Monument (c. 390-380 B.C.)

Greek temples (like this reconstruction of a temple-shaped tomb from Xanthos) were considered homes for the gods, with a statue of a god or goddess inside.

The triangle-shaped space above the columns—the pediment—is filled with sculpture. Supporting the pediment are decorative relief panels, called metopes. Now look through the columns to the building itself. Above the doorway, another set of relief panels—the frieze—runs around the building (under the eaves).

Next, we'll see pediment, frieze, and metope decorations from Greece's greatest temple.

▸ *Enter through the glass doors labeled Parthenon Galleries. (The rooms branching off the entryway usually have helpful exhibits that reconstruct the Parthenon and its once-colorful sculptures.)*

The Parthenon temple in Athens   Elgin Marbles—stripped from the Parthenon

㉗ Parthenon Galleries (447-432 B.C.)

The Parthenon—the temple dedicated to Athena, goddess of wisdom and the patroness of Athens—was the crowning glory of an enormous urban-renewal plan. After Athens was ruined in a war with Persia, the newly built Parthenon became the symbol of the Golden Age—a model of balance, simplicity, and harmonious elegance. Phidias, the greatest Greek sculptor, decorated the exterior with statues and relief panels.

While the building itself remains in Athens, many of the Parthenon's best sculptures are right here in the British Museum—the so-called Elgin Marbles, named for the shrewd British ambassador who had his men hammer, chisel, and saw them off the Parthenon in the early 1800s. Though the Greek government complains about losing its marbles, the Brits feel they rescued and preserved the sculptures. The often-bitter controversy continues.

The marble panels you see lining the walls of this large hall are part of the frieze that originally ran around the exterior of the Parthenon, under the eaves. The statues at either end of the hall once filled the Parthenon's triangular-shaped pediments. Near the pediment sculptures, we'll also find the relief panels known as metopes.

The Frieze

These 56 relief panels show Athens' "Fourth of July" parade, celebrating the birth of the city. On this day, citizens marched up the Acropolis to symbolically present a new robe to the 40-foot-tall gold-and-ivory statue of Athena housed in the Parthenon.

▶ *Start at the panels by the entrance (#136) and work counterclockwise.*

Men on horseback lead the parade, all heading in the same direction—uphill. Prance on.

Notice the muscles and veins in the horses' legs and the intricate folds in the cloaks and dresses. Some panels have holes drilled in them, where gleaming bronze reins were fitted to heighten the festive look. All these panels were originally painted in realistic colors. As you move along, notice that, despite the bustle of figures posed every which way, the frieze has one unifying element—all the people's heads are at the same level, creating a single ribbon around the Parthenon.

▶ Cross to the opposite wall.

A two-horse chariot (#67), cut from only a few inches of marble, is more lifelike and three-dimensional than anything the Egyptians achieved in a freestanding statue.

Enter the girls (five yards to the left, #61), the heart of the procession. Dressed in pleated robes, they shuffle past the parade marshals, carrying incense burners and jugs of wine and bowls to pour out an offering to the thirsty gods.

The procession culminates (#35) in the presentation of the robe to Athena. A man and a child fold the robe for the goddess while the rest of the gods look on. Zeus and Hera (#29), the king and queen of the gods,

Pediment—the gods lounge to the left...

seated, enjoy the fashion show and wonder what length hemlines will be this year.

▶ *Head for the set of pediment sculptures at the far right end of the hall.*

The Pediment Sculptures

These statues were originally nestled nicely in the triangular pediment above the columns at the Parthenon's main (east) entrance. The missing statues at the peak of the triangle once showed the birth of Athena. Zeus had his head split open, allowing Athena, the goddess of wisdom, to rise from his brain fully grown and fully armed, inaugurating the Golden Age of Athens.

The other gods at this Olympian banquet slowly become aware of the amazing event. Hebe, the cup-bearer of the gods (tallest surviving fragment) runs to tell the others, her dress whipping behind her. The only one who hasn't lost his head is laid-back Dionysus (the cool guy farther left). He just raises another glass of wine to his lips. Over on the right, Aphrodite, goddess of love, leans back into her mother's lap. A chess-set horse's head screams, "These people are nuts—let me out of here!"

The scene had a message. Just as wise Athena rose above the lesser gods, who were scared, drunk, or vain, so would her city, Athens, rise above her lesser rivals.

...and right of Athena's amazing birth

This is amazing workmanship. Compare Dionysus, with his natural, relaxed, reclining pose, to all those stiff Egyptian statues standing eternally at attention. Appreciate the intricate folds of the clothes on the female figures. Even without their heads, these statues, with their detailed anatomy and expressive poses, speak volumes.

▶ *The metopes are the panels on the walls to either side. Start with the three South Metope panels on the right wall, center.*

The Metopes

The Metopes depict the battle between humans and centaurs. Metaphorically, they tell the story of Greece's own struggle to rise above nomadic barbarism to the pinnacle of early Western civilization.

In #XXXI, a centaur grabs a man by the throat while the man pulls his hair. The humans have invited some centaurs—wild half-man/half-horse creatures—to a wedding feast. The centaurs, the original party animals, get too drunk and try to carry off the women. A battle ensues. In #XXX, the centaur does the hair-pulling, and begins to drive the man to his knees.

In #XXVIII (opposite wall, center), the centaurs take control of the party, as one rears back and prepares to trample the helpless man. The leopard skin draped over the centaur's arm roars a taunt. The humans lose face.

In #XXVII (to the left), the humans rally. A centaur tries to run, but the man grabs him by the neck and raises his (missing) right hand to run him through.

The centaurs have been defeated. Civilization has triumphed over barbarism, order over chaos, and rational man over his half-animal alter ego.

Why are the Parthenon sculptures so treasured? The British of the

Metope #XXXI—centaurs battle humans

#XXX—centaurs get the upper hand

Centaurs Slain Around the World

Dateline 500 B.C.—Greece, China, India: Man no longer considers himself an animal. Bold new ideas are exploding simultaneously around the world. Socrates, Confucius, Buddha, and others are independently discovering a nonmaterial, unseen order in nature and in man. They say man has a rational mind or soul. He's separate from nature and different from the other animals.

19th century saw themselves as the new "civilized" race, subduing "barbarians" in their far-flung empire. Maybe these rocks made them stop and wonder—will our great civilization also turn to rubble?

▶ *Our tour is over, but of course there's much more to the British Museum. Pick up the free map to find the 2,000-year-old Lindow Man (Room 50), Anglo-Saxon treasures (Room 41), a Michelangelo sketch (Room 90), and the elegant Enlightenment Gallery (Room 1). Look for remnants of the sophisticated, exotic cultures of Asia and the Americas (North Wing) and Africa (lower floor)—all part of the totem pole of the human family.*

#XXVIII—centaurs triumph

#XXVII—humans rally, defeating the barbarians

British Library Tour

The British Empire built its greatest monuments out of...paper. At the British Library, you'll see some of the many documents—literary, historical, and musical—that changed the course of history.

These national archives of Britain include more than 150 million items, 380 miles of shelving, and the deepest basement in London. But everything that matters for our visit is in one delightful room, where we'll focus on the highlights. We'll stand before old maps, ancient Bibles, Leonardo da Vinci's notebooks, the works of Shakespeare, highlights of English Lit 101, the Magna Carta, and—ladies and gentlemen—the Beatles.

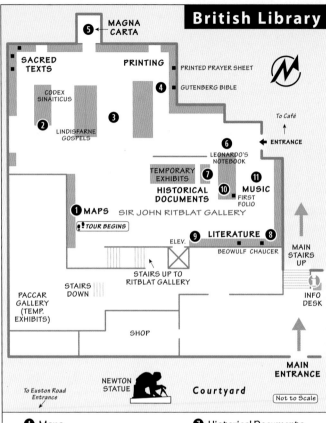

British Library

5 → MAGNA CARTA

SACRED TEXTS

PRINTING

■ PRINTED PRAYER SHEET

4 ■ GUTENBERG BIBLE

CODEX SINAITICUS

2

LINDISFARNE GOSPELS

3

To Café ↑

← ENTRANCE

LEONARDO'S NOTEBOOK

6

TEMPORARY EXHIBITS **7**

HISTORICAL DOCUMENTS

11 MUSIC

10 FIRST FOLIO

SIR JOHN RITBLAT GALLERY

1 MAPS

◉ TOUR BEGINS

ELEV.

9 **LITERATURE** **8**

■ BEOWULF CHAUCER

MAIN STAIRS UP

STAIRS UP TO RITBLAT GALLERY

STAIRS DOWN

PACCAR GALLERY (TEMP. EXHIBITS)

INFO DESK

SHOP

MAIN ENTRANCE

NEWTON STATUE

Courtyard

To Euston Road Entrance ↙

Not to Scale

1 Maps
2 Sacred Texts & Early Bibles
3 Art of the Book
4 Printing
5 Magna Carta
6 Leonardo da Vinci's Notebook

7 Historical Documents
8 English Literature
9 Shakespeare
10 The Beatles
11 Music

ORIENTATION

Cost: Free, but £5 suggested donation. Temporary exhibits may have a separate (optional) charge.

Hours: Mon-Fri 9:30-18:00, Tue-Thu until 20:00, Sat 9:30-17:00, Sun 11:00-17:00.

Getting There: It's at 96 Euston Road, a block west of Tube: King's Cross St. Pancras.

Information: Tel. 020/7412-7676. For questions on the collection, call 019/3754-6060 or go to www.bl.uk.

Tours: There are no guided tours or audioguides for the permanent collection. You can download this chapter as a free 🎧 Rick Steves audio tour (see page 201).

Length of This Tour: Allow one hour.

Cloakroom: Free. For security, bags may be searched at the library entrance.

Photography: No photos allowed.

Cuisine Art: The upper-level restaurant has good hot meals. The ground-floor café (sandwiches and drinks) is next to the vast and fun pull-out stamp collection.

Newton statue at the entrance—a symbol of knowledge

Starring: Bibles, Shakespeare, English Lit 101, Magna Carta, and—ladies and gentlemen—the Beatles.

THE TOUR BEGINS

Entering the library courtyard, you'll see a big statue of a naked Isaac Newton bending forward with a compass to measure the universe. The statue symbolizes the library's purpose: to gather all knowledge and promote our endless search for truth.

Stepping inside, you'll find our tour in a single, dimly lit room to the left. It's variously labeled "The Sir John Ritblat Gallery," "Treasures of the British Library," or just "The Treasures."

▶ *Enter and let your eyes adjust. The room has display cases grouped according to themes: maps, sacred texts, music, and so on. Focus on the big picture, and don't be too worried about locating every specific exhibit in this tour—the displays change often. Start at the far side of the room with the display case of...*

❶ Maps

The historic maps on the wall show how humans' perspective of the world expanded over the centuries. These pieces of paper, encoded with information gleaned from travelers, could be passed along to future generations—each building upon the knowledge of the last. You may see maps similar to these: A crude 13th-century map of Britain put medieval man in an unusual position—looking down on his homeland from 50 miles in the air. A few centuries later, maps of Britain were of such high quality they could be used today to plan a trip. And only a few generations after Columbus' first journey, the entire globe was fairly well-mapped, except for the mysterious expanse of unknown land that lay beyond America's east coast—"Terra Incognita."

▶ *Move into the area dedicated to sacred texts from several cultures—the Hebrew Torah, Muslim Quran, Buddhist sutras, and Hindu Upanishads. Start by browsing the different versions of the sacred text of Christians, the Bible.*

❷ Sacred Texts (including Early Bibles)

My favorite excuse for not learning a foreign language is "If English was

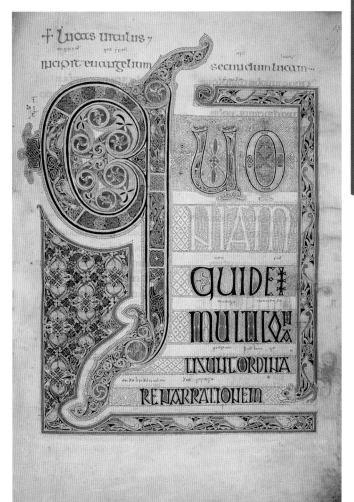

Lindisfarne Gospels—copied and illustrated by monks

good enough for Jesus Christ, it's good enough for me!" I don't know what that has to do with anything, but obviously Jesus didn't speak English—nor did Moses or Isaiah or Paul or any other Bible authors or characters. As a result, our present-day English Bible came not directly from the mouths and pens of these religious figures, but is instead the fitful product of centuries of evolution and translation.

There are three things that editors must do in compiling the most accurate Bible: 1) decide which writings belong in the "anthology," 2) find the oldest and most accurate version (usually written in Hebrew or Greek), and 3) translate it accurately.

The **Codex Sinaiticus,** from A.D. 350, is one of the oldest complete Bibles in existence ("codex" means it's an ancient, bound manuscript). It's in Greek, the language in which most of the New Testament was written. The Old Testament portions are Greek translations from the original Hebrew. This particular Bible, and the nearby **Codex Alexandrinus** (A.D. 425), are old, but even they date from long after Jesus' death. Today, Bible scholars pore diligently over every word in the New Testament, trying to separate Jesus' authentic words from those that seem to have been added later.

❸ Art of the Book

During Europe's Dark Ages, after the fall of Rome, the Christian message was preserved by monks, who painstakingly reproduced ancient Bibles by hand. They wrote in Latin, the language of scholars ever since the Roman Empire. The **Lindisfarne Gospels** (A.D. 698) is the most magnificent of medieval British monk-uscripts. It's beautifully illustrated, or "illuminated," with elaborate tracery and interwoven decoration, mixing Irish, classical, and even Byzantine forms.

These Gospels are a reminder that Christianity almost didn't make it in Europe. After the fall of Rome (which had established Christianity as the empire's official religion), much of Europe reverted to its pagan, tree-worshipping ways. Monasteries like the one at Lindisfarne (an island off the east coast of England) were the few beacons of light, tending the embers of civilization through the long night of the Dark Ages. While browsing the displays in Art of the Book (and in Sacred Texts), you'll likely see some **Early English Bibles.**

By the year 1400, the Bible was still written in Latin, even though only a small percentage of the population understood that language. A few brave reformers risked death to translate the sacred books into English.

These Bibles are written in the same language you speak, but try reading them. The strange letters and archaic words clearly show how quickly languages evolve. Jesus spoke Aramaic, a form of Hebrew. His words were written down in Greek. Greek manuscripts were translated into Latin, the language of medieval monks and scholars. In the 1400s, English scholars began translating the Greek and Latin into the King's English.

The **King James version** (made during his reign) has been the most widely used English translation. Fifty scholars worked for four years, borrowing heavily from previous translations, to produce the work. Its impact on the English language was enormous. It made Elizabethan English something of the standard, even after ordinary people had long since stopped saying "thee," "thou," and "verily, verily."

❹ Printing (c. 1455)

Printing was invented by the Chinese (what wasn't?). The **Printed Prayer Sheet** (c. 618-907) was printed using wooden blocks carved with Chinese characters, then dipped into paint or ink.

Johann Gutenberg (c. 1397-1468), a German silversmith, improved on the process. The **Gutenberg Bible** was the first book printed in Europe using movable type, one of the most revolutionary inventions in history.

Here's how it works: You scratch each letter onto a separate metal block, then arrange them into words, ink them up, and press them onto paper. When one job was done you could reuse the same letters for a new one.

Suddenly, the Bible was available for anyone to read, fueling the Protestant Reformation. Secular knowledge became accessible to a wide

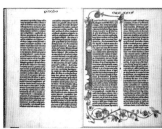
Gutenberg's press put monks out of work.

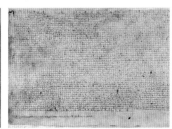
The Magna Carta established "due process."

audience, fueling the Renaissance. Books were the mass medium of Europe, linking people by a common set of ideas.

❺ Magna Carta (1215)

Duck into the Magna Carta Room to answer this question: How did Britain, a tiny island with a few million people, come to rule a quarter of the world? Not by force, but by law. The Magna Carta was the basis for England's constitutional system of government. Though historians talk about "the" Magna Carta, several different versions of the document exist, some of which are kept in this room.

In 1215, England's barons rose in revolt against the slimy King John. (Remember, John appears as a villain in the legends of Robin Hood.) After losing London, John was forced to negotiate. The barons presented him with this list of demands. John, whose rule was worthless without the barons' support, had no choice but to affix his seal to it. Some 35 copies of the "Great Charter" were distributed around the kingdom.

This was a turning point in the history of government. Now, for the first time, there were limits—in writing—on how a king could treat his subjects. More generally, it established the idea of "due process"—the notion that a government can't infringe on citizens' freedom without a legitimate legal reason. This small step became the basis for all constitutional governments, including yours.

So what did this radical piece of paper actually say? The specific demands were trivial by today's standards—the king's duties to widows and orphans, inheritance taxes, and so on. But the principle—that the king had to abide by them as law—was revolutionary.

▶ *Now return to the main room to find...*

❻ Leonardo da Vinci's Notebook

As books spread secular knowledge, Renaissance men turned their attention away from heaven and toward the nuts and bolts of the material world around them. These pages from Leonardo's notebook show his powerful curiosity, his genius for invention, and his famous backward and inside-out handwriting, which makes sense only if you know Italian and have a mirror. Leonardo's restless mind pondered diverse subjects, from how birds fly to the flow of the Arno River to military fortifications to an early helicopter to the "earthshine" reflecting onto the moon.

One person's research inspired another's, and books allowed

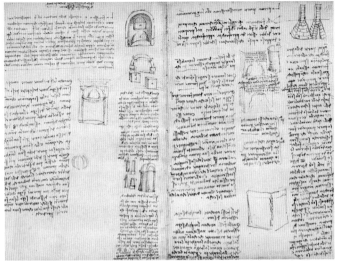
Leonardo's notebook: You'd need a mirror to read the ingenious inventor's backward writing.

knowledge to accumulate. Leonardo inspired Galileo, who championed the counter-commonsense notion that the earth spun around the sun. Galileo inspired Isaac Newton, who perfected the mathematics of those moving celestial bodies.

❼ Historical Documents

Nearby are many more historical documents. The displays change frequently, but you may see letters by Henry VIII, Queen Elizabeth I, Darwin, Freud, Gandhi, and others. But for now, let's trace the evolution of...

❽ English Literature

Ponder this first English literary masterpiece, **Beowulf.** The manuscript is from A.D. 1000, although the story itself dates to about A.D. 750. In this Anglo-Saxon epic poem, the young hero Beowulf defeats two half-human monsters threatening the kingdom. Beowulf symbolizes England's emergence from the chaos and barbarism of the Dark Ages.

The poem is written in Old English, a language indecipherable to us today. Modern English is a mix derived from the various people who've inhabited the island: Celtic tribesmen, Latin-speaking Romans, German-speaking Anglos and Saxons (who named the island "Angle-land"—England), Vikings from Denmark, and French-speaking Normans under William the Conqueror. Four out of every five English words have been borrowed from other languages.

Six hundred years later, the island's inhabitants spoke Middle English. While most serious literature of the time was written in scholarly Latin, *The Canterbury Tales* **(c. 1410)** were written in the people's tongue. Geoffrey Chaucer's bawdy collection of stories, told by pilgrims on their way to Canterbury, gives us the full range of life's experiences—happy, sad, silly, sexy, and devout.

The rest of the Literature wall is a greatest-hits sampling of British literature, featuring works that have enlightened and brightened our lives for centuries. The displays rotate frequently, but there's always a tasty selection of famous works, from Brontë to Kipling to Woolf to Joyce to Dickens, whose novels were as popular in his time as blockbuster movies are today. In the 21st century, Britain continues to be a powerful force in the world of ideas and imagination.

⑨ Shakespeare (1564-1616)

William Shakespeare is the greatest author in any language. Period. He expanded and helped define modern English. In one fell swoop, he made the language of everyday people as important as Latin. In the process, he gave us phrases like "one fell swoop," which we quote without knowing they're Shakespeare.

Perhaps as important was his insight into humanity. Think of his stock of great characters and great lines: Hamlet ("To be or not to be, that is the question"), Othello and his jealousy ("It is the green-eyed monster"), ambitious Mark Antony ("Friends, Romans, countrymen, lend me your ears"), rowdy Falstaff ("The better part of valor is discretion"), and the star-crossed lovers Romeo and Juliet ("But soft, what light through yonder window breaks"). Shakespeare probed the psychology of human beings 300 years before Freud. Even today, his characters strike a familiar chord.

The Shakespeare First Folio (1623): This published collection of his plays was the first authorized version. Shakespeare wrote his plays to be performed, not read. But as his reputation grew, unauthorized "bootleg"

Shakespeare, from the First Folio

Handel's *Messiah*

versions began to circulate. Some of these were shoddy, written by actors who were trying to re-create plays they had appeared in years before.

This folio, edited by friends and fellow actors, came out seven years after Shakespeare's death.

The title page has an engraving of Shakespeare, one of only two portraits done during his lifetime. The shiny, domed forehead is a beacon of intelligence. Is this what he really looked like? No one knows. The best answer probably comes from Ben Jonson, in the introduction on the facing page. Jonson concludes, "Reader, look not on his picture, but his book."

⑩ The Beatles

Bach, Beethoven, Brahms, Bizet...Beatles. Future generations will have to judge whether this musical quartet ranks with such artists, but no one can deny their historical significance. The Beatles burst onto the scene in the early 1960s to unheard-of popularity. With their long hair and loud music, they brought counterculture and revolutionary ideas to the middle class, affecting the values of a whole generation. Touring the globe, they served as a link between young people everywhere. Look for photos of John Lennon, Paul McCartney, George Harrison, and Ringo Starr before and after their fame.

Most interesting are the manuscripts of song lyrics written by Lennon and McCartney, the two guiding lights of the group. "I Want to Hold Your Hand" was the song that launched them to superstardom. "A Hard Day's Night" and "Help" were title songs of two films capturing the excitement and chaos of their hectic touring schedule. Some call "A Ticket to Ride" the first heavy-metal song. "Michelle," with a line in French, seemed

The Beatles captured the exuberant spirit of rebellious Baby Boomers across the globe.

oh-so-sophisticated. "Yesterday," by Paul, was recorded with guitar and voice backed by a string quartet—a touch of class from producer George Martin. Also, glance at the rambling, depressed, and cynical but humorous "untitled verse" by a young John Lennon. Is that a self-portrait at the bottom?

⑪ Music

Kind of an anticlimax after the Fab Four, I know, but here are manuscripts by Mozart, Beethoven, Schubert, and others. George Frideric Handel's famous oratorio, the **Messiah** (1741), is often on display. It was written in a flash of inspiration—three hours of music in 24 days. Here are the final bars of its most famous tune.

    Hallelujah.

Tower of London Tour

William I, still getting used to his new title of "the Conqueror," built a castle tower here (1077-1097) to keep the Londoners in line. Over the centuries, his successors built more walls and towers around it to create this complex, which today covers 18 acres. The heavily fortified Tower served as a royal residence, the Royal Mint, the Royal Jewel House, and, most famously, as the prison and execution site of those who dared oppose the Crown.

The Tower represents the ultimate power of the monarch. See the execution site where Henry VIII axed exes. Ogle the crown jewels, the richest on earth. See prisons that held the likes of Sir Walter Raleigh, Queen Elizabeth, and the Nazi Rudolf Hess. Tour halls of armor and weapons and take a meaty Beefeater tour. You'll find more bloody history per square inch than anywhere else in Britain by touring this original tower of power.

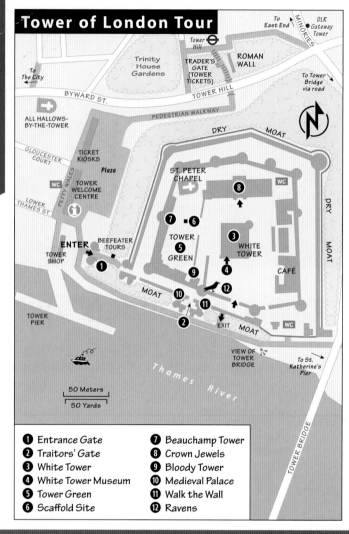

Tower of London Tour

To East End
To
DLR Gateway Tower

Tower Hill

Trinity House Gardens

TRADER'S GATE (TOWER TICKETS)

ROMAN WALL

To The City

BYWARD ST.

TOWER HILL

To Tower Bridge via road

PEDESTRIAN WALKWAY

ALL HALLOWS-BY-THE-TOWER

DRY MOAT

N

GLOUCESTER COURT

TICKET KIOSKS

Plaza

WC

TOWER WELCOME CENTRE

ST. PETER CHAPEL

WC

DRY MOAT

LOWER THAMES ST.

PETTY WALES

7 6

8

ENTER

BEEFEATER TOURS

TOWER GREEN

3

WHITE TOWER

TOWER SHOP

1

5

4

9

CAFÉ

MOAT

10

12

11

2

EXIT   MOAT

WC

TOWER PIER

VIEW OF TOWER BRIDGE

To St. Katherine's Pier

Thames River

50 Meters

50 Yards

TOWER BRIDGE

1 Entrance Gate
2 Traitors' Gate
3 White Tower
4 White Tower Museum
5 Tower Green
6 Scaffold Site
7 Beauchamp Tower
8 Crown Jewels
9 Bloody Tower
10 Medieval Palace
11 Walk the Wall
12 Ravens

ORIENTATION

Cost: £25, family-£63 (2 adults plus up to 3 kids ages 5-15).

Hours: March-Oct Tue-Sat 9:00-17:30, Sun-Mon 10:00-17:30; Nov closes one hour earlier.

Advance Tickets: To avoid the long ticket-buying lines, buy your ticket at the Trader's Gate gift shop, located at the Tower Hill Tube stop. (As you exit the station, go down a flight of steps—the low-profile souvenir store is tucked away at the foot of the stairs.) Tickets are also sold at other locations (such as travel agencies) in London. Or you can buy tickets at the Tower Welcome Centre (to the left of the normal ticket lines, credit card only), by phone (tel. 0844-482-7788 within UK or tel. 011-44-20-3166-6000 from the US, £2 fee), or online (www.hrp.org. uk, 10 percent discount, no fee, ticket valid on any day up to 7 days after visitation date you select online.

More Crowd-Beating Tips: It's most crowded in summer, on weekends (especially Sun), and during school holidays. Avoid lines at the always crowded crown jewels by visiting before 10:00 or shortly before closing.

Getting There: The Tower is located in East London (Tube: Tower Hill). Thames Clipper boats make the pleasant 45-minute trip from Westminster Pier near Big Ben.

Information: Switchboard tel. 0844-482-7788, www.hrp.org.uk.

Yeoman Warder (Beefeater) Tours: Free, one-hour Beefeater tours leave about every 30 minutes from inside the gate (first tour Tue-Sat at 10:00, Sun-Mon at 10:30, last tour at 15:30, 14:30 in winter). The boisterous Beefeaters are great entertainers, focusing on bloody anecdotes.

Length of This Tour: Allow two hours.

Photography: Photos are allowed, except of the jewels or in the chapels.

Eating: The $$ New Armouries Café, inside the Tower, is a big, efficient cafeteria (large, splittable meals). Outside the Tower, there's a row of fast-food joints along the river and behind the Welcome Centre, and various $ takeout stands. Picnicking is allowed on the Tower grounds.

Starring: The crown jewels, Beefeaters, William the Conqueror, and Henry VIII.

THE TOUR BEGINS

❶ Entrance Gate

Even an army the size of the ticket line couldn't storm this castle. After the drawbridge was pulled up and the iron portcullis slammed down, you'd have to swim a 120-foot moat; cross an island prowled by wild animals; then toss a grappling hook onto a wall and climb up while the enemy poured boiling oil on you. If you made it this far, you'd only be halfway there.

You'd still have to swim a second moat—eventually drained to make the grassy parade ground we see today—then, finally, scale a second, higher wall. In all, the central tower was surrounded by two concentric rings of walls. Yes, it was difficult to get into the Tower (if you were a foreign enemy)...but it was almost as impossible to get out (if you were an enemy of the state).

▶ *Show your ticket, enter, pick up a free map, and check the posted schedule of Beefeater tours and daily events. When you're all set, go 50 yards straight ahead to the...*

❷ Traitors' Gate

This was the boat entrance to the Tower from the Thames. Princess Elizabeth, who was a prisoner here before she became Queen Elizabeth I, was carried down the Thames and through this gate on a barge, thinking about her mom, Anne Boleyn, who had been decapitated inside just a few years earlier. Many English leaders who fell from grace entered through here—Elizabeth was one of the lucky few to walk out.

▶ *Continue straight and turn left to pass underneath the archway just*

Some of the Tower's many ramparts

Traitors' Gate—the boat entrance

The Beefeaters

The original duty of the Yeoman Warders (called "Beefeaters") was to guard the Tower, its prisoners, and the jewels. Their nickname may come from an original perk of the job—large rations of the king's beef. The Beefeaters dress in blue knee-length coats with red trim and a top hat. The "ER" on the chest stands for the  monarch they serve—Queen Elizabeth II (Elizabetha Regina in Latin). On special occasions, they wear red. All are retired noncommissioned officers from the armed forces with distinguished service records.

These days, the Yeoman Warders are entertaining tour guides. There are 35 Yeoman Warders, including one woman. They and their families make for a Beefeating community of 120 that live inside the Tower.

before the cannons (opposite the exit), which leads into the inner courtyard. The big, white tower in the middle is the...

❸ White Tower

This square, 90-foot-tall tower is the original structure built by William the Conqueror that gave this castle complex of 20 towers its name. In the 13th century, the tower was painted white, hence the name.

Standing high above the rest of old London, the White Tower provided a gleaming reminder of the monarch's absolute power over subjects. If you made the wrong move here, you could be feasting on roast boar in the banqueting hall one night and chained to the walls of the prison the next. Torture ranged from stretching on the rack to the full Monty: hanging by the neck until nearly dead, then "drawing" (cut open to be gutted), and finally quartering, with your giblets displayed on the walls as a warning. Any cries for help were muffled by the thick stone walls—15 feet at the base.

▶ *Either now or later, find time to go inside the White Tower for its excellent museum.*

The White Tower—the oldest of the Tower's towers—stands in the middle of the walled complex.

❹ White Tower Museum

Inside the White Tower, a one-way route winds through exhibits re-creating medieval life and the Tower's bloody history of torture and executions.

You'll see several suits of armor of Henry VIII—seated on horseback, slender in his youth (c. 1515), heavy-set by 1540—with his bigger-is-better codpiece. Upstairs, the rare and lovely St. John's Chapel (1080) is where Lady Jane Grey (described later) offered up a last unanswered prayer. The Arsenal displays the heaviest suit of armor in the world (130 pounds!), as well as weapons used through the ages, including machine guns and the jeweled "Tiffany Revolver." On the top floor: There it is—the Tower's actual chopping block and execution ax.

▸ *Back outside, find the courtyard to the left of the White Tower, called...*

❺ Tower Green

This spacious courtyard within the walls was once the "town square" for those who lived in the castle. Knights exercised and jousted here, residents worshipped at the stone Chapel Royal of St. Peter ad Vincula (north side), and this was the last place of refuge in troubled times. The Tower is still officially a royal residence: The Queen's lodgings are on the south side of the green, in the white half-timbered buildings where a soldier stands guard.

▸ *Near the middle of Tower Green is a granite-paved square marked* Site of Scaffold.

❻ Scaffold Site

The actual execution site looks pleasant enough today; the chopping block has been moved to inside the White Tower, and a modern sculpture encourages visitors to ponder those who died.

The White Tower Museum displays armaments.

The executioner's ax

Here, enemies of the Crown would kneel before the king for the final time. With their hands tied behind their backs, they would say a final prayer, lay their heads on a block, and then—*shlit*—the blade would slice through their necks, their heads tumbling to the ground. The headless corpses were buried in unmarked graves in Tower Green or under the floor of the Chapel Royal of St. Peter ad Vincula. The heads were stuck on a stick and displayed at London Bridge. Passersby did not see heads, but rather spheres covered with insects and parasites.

Tower Green was the most prestigious execution site. Common criminals were hanged outside the Tower. More prominent evil-doers were decapitated before jeering crowds atop Tower Hill (near today's Tube station). Inside the Tower walls was reserved for the most heinous traitors.

Henry VIII axed a couple of his ex-wives here. (Divorced readers can insert their own cynical joke.) Anne Boleyn was the appealing young woman Henry had fallen so hard for that he broke with the Catholic Church in order to divorce his first wife and marry her. But when Anne failed to produce a male heir, she was locked up in the Tower, branded an adulteress and traitor, and decapitated.

Henry's fifth wife, teenage Catherine Howard, was also beheaded here. So was Jane Boleyn (Anne's sister-in-law) for arranging Catherine's adulterous affair behind Henry's back. Next.

In 1554, 17-year-old Lady Jane Grey—who'd been manipulated into claiming the Crown—was executed here by her cousin Queen ("Bloody") Mary I. Young Jane had watched as her husband was decapitated hours earlier. Jane bravely blindfolded herself, hoping for a dignified end. But then she couldn't find the chopping block. She crawled around the scaffold pleading "Where is it?!" A bystander graciously helped her find it, thankfully avoiding a dreadful faux pas.

Tower Green—the complex's courtyard

Execution site—Anne Boleyn died here

Years ago, a Beefeater, tired of the "Hollywood coverage" of the Tower, told me that in more than 900 years, only 120 were executed here, and, of those, only six were executed inside the walls. Stressing the hospitality of the Tower, they insist that "Torture was actually quite rare here."

▶ *Overlooking the scaffold site is the...*

❼ Beauchamp Tower—Prisoners

The Beauchamp Tower (pronounced "BEECH-um") was one of several places in the complex that housed Very Important Prisoners. In an upstairs room, you can read graffiti carved into the stone by bored and despondent inmates.

Picture Philip Howard, the Earl of Arundel (c. 1555-1595), warming himself by this fireplace and glancing out at the execution site during his 10-year incarceration. On June 22, 1587, he carved his family name "Arundell" into the chimney (graffiti #13) and wrote in Latin, *Quanto plus afflictionis*—"The more we suffer for Christ in this world, the more glory with Christ in the next."

Read other pitiful graffiti. Graffiti #85 belongs to Lady Jane Grey's young husband, Lord Guilford Dudley. Locked in the Beauchamp Tower and executed the same day as his wife, Dudley vented his despair by scratching "IANE" into the stone. Many prisoners held onto their sense of identity by carving their family's coats of arms.

The last enemy of state imprisoned in the Tower complex was one of its most infamous: the renegade Nazi Rudolf Hess. In 1941, Hitler's henchman secretly flew to Britain with a peace proposal (Hitler denied any such plan). He parachuted into a field, was arrested and held for four days in the Tower, and was later given a life sentence for war crimes.

▶ *Join the line leading to the crown jewels. Like a line for a Disney ride, the queue is still quite long even once you've made it in the door. But great videos help pass the time. They show close-ups of the jewels and how they've been used during centuries of coronations, including Queen Elizabeth II's in 1953. After passing a hallway of ceremonial maces, swords, and trumpets, you finally reach the...*

❽ Crown Jewels

The first displays show the royal regalia. The monarch-to-be is anointed with holy oil poured from the eagle-beak flask, dressed in the 20-pound gold robe, and handed the jeweled sword. The 12th-century coronation spoon, last used in 1953 to anoint the head of Queen Elizabeth, is the

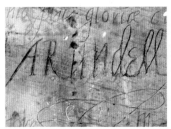

Prisoners left pitiful messages.

The crown jewels

most ancient object here. Most of the original crown jewels from medieval times were lost during Cromwell's 1648 revolution. After being dressed and anointed, the new monarch prepares for the "crowning" moment.

▶ *Five glass cases display the various crowns, orbs, and scepters used in various royal ceremonies. Ride the moving sidewalk that takes you past them. You're welcome to circle back and glide by again, or hang out on the elevated viewing area. The displays change often, but the following items are generally on display.*

Scepter and Orb: After being crowned, the new monarch is handed these items. The Sovereign's Scepter is encrusted with the world's largest cut diamond—the 530-carat Star of Africa, beefy as a quarter-pounder. This was one of nine stones cut from the original 3,106-carat (1.37-pound) Cullinan diamond. The orb symbolizes how Christianity rules over the earth. The monarch is head of both the state and the Church of England.

St. Edward's Crown: This coronation crown is the one placed by the archbishop upon the head of each new monarch on coronation day in Westminster Abbey. It's worn for 20 minutes, then locked away until the next coronation. The original crown, destroyed by Cromwell, was older than the Tower itself and dated back to 1061, the time of King Edward the Confessor, "the last English king" before William the Conqueror invaded from France (1066). This 1661 remake is said to contain some of the original's gold amid its 443 precious and semiprecious stones. Because the crown weighs nearly five pounds, weak or frail monarchs have opted not to wear it.

Other Crowns: Among the several crowns, notice how four-arch crowns are for monarchs, while princes get only two. **The Crown of the Queen Mother** has the 106-carat Koh-I-Noor diamond glittering on the front. The **Queen Victoria Small Diamond Crown** is tiny, because it was designed to sit atop Victoria's widow's veil. The impressive **Imperial State Crown** is what the Queen wears for official functions. It's the crown depicted on Britain's coins and stamps. Among its 3,733 jewels are Queen Elizabeth I's former earrings (the hanging pearls, top center), and a blue sapphire (on top) from the ring of King Edward the Confessor.

▶ *Leave the jewels by exiting through the thick vault doors and head back toward the Scaffold Site. Find the entrance to the Bloody Tower at the far end of Tower Green.*

❾ Bloody Tower

Not all prisoners died at the block. The 13-year-old King Edward V and his kid brother were kidnapped in 1483 during the Wars of the Roses by their uncle Richard III ("Now is the winter of our discontent...") and locked in the Bloody Tower, never to be seen again. (End of story? Two centuries later, the skeletons of two children were found here.) Sir Walter Raleigh (c.1554-1618)—poet, explorer, and political radical—was imprisoned here for 13 years, accused of plotting against King James. While in the Bloody Tower, Raleigh wrote the first volume of his *History of the World.* Check out his rather cushy bedroom, study, and walkway (courtesy of the powerful tobacco lobby?).

▶ *To reach the next sight, exit through the Bloody Gate, cross the cobbled road, and bear right a few steps to find the stairs up onto the wall.*

❿ Medieval Palace

The Tower was a royal residence as well as a fortress. These rooms were built around 1240 by Henry III, the king most responsible for the expansive

View of Tower (not "London") Bridge

A "knight" regales tourists near the ramparts.

Tower of London complex we see today. You'll see the king's re-created bedroom and throne room, both with massive fireplaces to keep this cold stone palace cozy.

▶ *From the throne room, continue up the stairs to...*

⑪ Walk the Wall

Strolling the ramparts, you get a good look at the 13th century's state-of-the-art fortifications. You can also see the famous Tower Bridge, with the twin towers and blue spans. Although it looks somewhat medieval, this drawbridge was built in 1894 of steel and concrete. Sophisticated steam engines raise and lower the bridge, allowing tall ships to squeeze through.

Gaze out at the bridge, the river, City Hall (the egg-shaped glass building across the river), the Shard skyscraper (the city's bold exclamation point), and life-filled London.

▶ *Between the White Tower and the Bloody Tower are cages housing the...*

⑫ Ravens

According to goofy tradition, the Tower and British throne are only safe as long as the ravens are here. Their wings are clipped so they'll stay, and about eight are kept in the cage. World War II bombing raids reduced the population to one. In recent years, with their clipped wings, the birds had trouble mating, so a slide was built to help them get a bit of lift to mate. Happily, that worked, and a baby raven was born.

▶ *Take one final look at the stern stone walls of the Tower. Be glad you can leave.*

Sights

London offers more world-class sights and museums than anyone could see in a single visit. To help you prioritize your limited time and money, I've clustered London's top sights into walkable neighborhoods for more efficient sightseeing. In the Westminster neighborhood, for example, you could string together a great day of sightseeing, linking Big Ben, Westminster Abbey, the Churchill War Rooms, and much more. You'll find a full day's worth of sights in the West End, The City, the South Bank, and other neighborhoods.

Remember that some of London's biggest sights (marked with a ✪) are described in detail in the individual walks and tours chapters. A 🎧 means the sight is available as a free audio tour (via my Rick Steves Audio Europe app—see page 201). See the Practicalities chapter for sightseeing tips.

And finally, remember that—although London's sights can be crowded and stressful—the city itself is all about gentility and grace under pressure. Be flexible.

CENTRAL LONDON

Westminster

In the shadow of Big Ben and Parliament, the Westminster neighborhood is Britain's government center. Most tourist sights lie in a half-mile stretch between Big Ben/Parliament (Tube: Westminster) and Trafalgar Square (Tube: Charing Cross).

▲▲Big Ben and the Houses of Parliament (Palace of Westminster)

This icon of London is where the British government's legislative branch meets. Big Ben, the 315-foot-high clock tower at the north end of the Houses of Parliament, is named for its 13-ton bell, Ben. (✪ For more on Big Ben, see page 15.) Tourists can enter the Houses of Parliament when Parliament is in session to see the impressive interior and view debates in either the bickering House of Commons or the genteel House of Lords.

The Houses of Parliament have been the center of political power in England for nearly a thousand years—first as a royal residence (1042-1547), then as home to the increasingly powerful Parliament. In 1834, a horrendous fire gutted the palace. It was rebuilt in a Neo-Gothic style of pointed arches, stained-glass windows, spires, and saint-like statues. Today, "Westminster" (as Brits call the place) appears almost nightly on TV, as the impressive backdrop to the latest political news.

Westminster Hall—covering 16,000 square feet—survived the 1834 fire, and is one of the oldest (from 1097) and most important structures in England. Its self-supporting oak-timber "hammer-beam" roof uses a complex system of curved braces and arches that distribute the weight of the roof outward, so there's no need for supporting pillars. It was in this historic hall that the king once presided on his throne, where England's vaunted legal system was developed, and where King Charles I was sentenced to death. In more recent times, the hall has hosted the lying-in-state of Winston Churchill and a speech by Barack Obama.

St. Stephen's Hall is where visitors wait to enter the House of Commons. This long, beautifully lit room was the original House of Commons for three centuries (from 1550 until the fire of 1834). After the fire, the hall was rebuilt. The stained-glass windows—forming a tall, rectangular grid—are a textbook example of the "Perpendicular" Gothic style used by architect Charles Barry. Next, you reach the **Central Lobby,** where visitors wait to visit the House of Lords (this is where the term "lobbying" comes from). This octagonal, high-vaulted room is often called the "heart of British government," because it sits in the geographical center of the sprawling, 1,100-room palace.

The **Lords Chamber** (which you view from an upper-level gallery) is church-like and impressive, with stained glass, intricately carved walls, and red-upholstered benches. At the far end is the Queen's gilded throne. The House of Lords consists of about 800 members, who are not elected by popular vote. Some are nobles who've inherited the position, others are appointed by the Queen. These days, their role is advisory; they have no real power to pass laws on their own.

The **Commons Chamber** is much less grandiose, but this is where the sausage gets made. The House of Commons is as powerful as the Lords, prime minister, and Queen combined. Some 650-plus Members of Parliament assemble on the green-upholstered benches to debate and pass laws. The ruling party is to the left, and the opposition to the right, with the canopied Speaker's Chair in between. The table in the center has two wooden chests that serve as lecterns, one for each side. The Chamber is at its liveliest when the prime minister visits (usually on Wed) to

The Houses of Parliament's vast Westminster Hall, with its ingenious wooden roof

stand at the lectern and defend her policies, while the opposition grumbles and harrumphs in displeasure.

▶ *Parliament is open for visitors (and always free of charge) whenever Parliament is in session—generally Oct to late July, Mon-Thu. The House of Commons is in session Mon 14:30-22:30, Tue-Wed 11:30-19:30, Thu 9:30-17:30; House of Lords in session Mon-Tue 14:30-22:00, Wed 15:00-22:00, Thu 11:00-19:30; last entry depends on the debates, both houses closed Fri-Sun except for Sat tours. Get the exact schedule for your visit to London from the parliament website (www.parliament.uk). During the late July-Sept recess, the only way to visit is on a guided tour (£25.50, generally Mon-Sat, book ahead by calling 0844-847-1672 or through www.ticketmaster.co.uk). Tube: Westminster, tel. 020/7219-4272 or 020/7219-3107, www.parliament.uk.*

To avoid the hour-plus waits for the House of Commons, consider queuing up for the less-crowded House of Lords. (Once inside, you can switch.) All visitors must pass through security and be photographed. The later in the day you enter, the less crowded (and less exciting) it is.

▲▲▲Westminster Abbey

The greatest church in the English-speaking world, Westminster Abbey is the place where England's kings and queens have been crowned and buried since 1066.

✪ For a self-guided tour of Westminster Abbey, see page 27.

▲▲▲Churchill War Rooms

In the darkest days of World War II—with Nazi bombs raining down on a helpless London and invasion imminent—Britain's government hunkered down in this underground headquarters to direct the war effort. It was here that Prime Minister Winston Churchill lived, worked, and made stirring radio speeches that inspired Brits to carry on.

Today you can tour the well-preserved, 27-room, heavily fortified nerve center of the war effort from 1939 to 1945. See Churchill's room, the map room, and other offices, while listening to recordings of first-person accounts. You'll see how British gentility survived even as the city was bombarded.

The Churchill Museum dissects every aspect of the man behind the famous cigar, bowler hat, and V-for-victory sign. You get a taste of Winston's wit, irascibility, work ethic, passion for painting, American

Churchill War Rooms—a WWII underground HQ   Banqueting House—colorful Rubens ceiling

connections, writing talents, and drinking habits. It traces the varied stages of his long life (1874-1965): newspaper reporter, war hero, Conservative politician, Liberal politician, and author. In the 1930s, he was a political pariah for ranting about the growing threat of Hitler's fascism. When his vision proved right, he was appointed prime minister on the day Hitler invaded the Netherlands. After the war, it was Churchill who warned of the Soviet threat, coining the phrase "Iron Curtain." Touring this place, you have to wonder how different the world might have been today without Winston Churchill.

▶ *£19.00, includes excellent audioguide. Open daily 9:30-18:00, last entry one hour before closing. Located on King Charles Street, 200 yards off Whitehall (Tube: Westminster). Food at the $$ café inside or the Westminster Arms Pub two blocks south on Storey's Gate. Tel. 020/7930-6961, www.iwm.org.uk/churchill.*

▲Banqueting House

England's first classical-style building (1619-1622) has an impressive great hall topped with ceiling paintings by Peter Paul Rubens. Built as the dining hall and de facto throne room for King James I, it symbolized his "divine right" management style—the belief that God had anointed him to rule. The hall is the only highlight of the visit—at 55 feet wide, 55 feet high, and 110 feet long, it's a perfect double cube. The large, colorful ceiling paintings (up to 28 feet by 20 feet) portray James I as king of the whole world, crowned by Greek gods who bless him. The Banqueting House's most famous role was as the place where James' son, Charles I, was executed—and divine-right rule ended. Today, it's a rent-a-hall hosting government receptions and concerts.

▶ *£8, includes audioguide. Fri-Wed 10:00-17:00, closed Thu, may close for government functions. Located along Whitehall (Tube: Westminster). Tel. 020/3166-6155, www.hrp.org.uk.*

✪ *For more on the exterior, see page 22 in the Westminster Walk chapter.*

On Trafalgar Square

▲▲Trafalgar Square

London's recently renovated square is arguably the center of the vast city of London.

✪ See page 24 in the Westminster Walk chapter.

▲▲▲National Gallery

Britain's top collection of paintings is also one of the world's greatest collections—a microcosm of European art history, from medieval to Michelangelo to Monet and Van Gogh.

✪ See the National Gallery Tour chapter.

▲▲National Portrait Gallery

Rock groupies, book lovers, movie fans, gossipmongers, and even historians all can find at least one favorite celebrity here. From Elizabeth I to Elizabeth II, Byron to Bowie, and Brontës to Beatles, the National Portrait Gallery is a *Who's Who* of 500 years of Britain's most fascinating people.

You'll see an imposing Henry VIII and several of his wives. Three different portraits of Elizabeth I offer multiple perspectives on the "Virgin Queen." William Shakespeare appears less as a stuffy scholar than a bohemian barfly. You'll see Charles I with his head on, Queen Victoria with her husband, writers in the throes of inspiration, and many scientists and philosophers who've changed the world.

The collection brings you right up to today, with sometimes-quirky portraits of the film stars, writers, and musicians that continue to make Britain great.

▶ *Free, but suggested donation of £5, optional temporary exhibits extra. Open daily 10:00-18:00, Thu-Fri until 21:00, first and second floors open Mon at 11:00. Well-done £3 themed audioguides. The entrance is 100 yards off Trafalgar Square (Tube: Charing Cross or Leicester Square). Tel. 020/7306-0055, recorded info tel. 020/7312-2463, www.npg.org.uk.*

▲St. Martin-in-the-Fields

The church, built in the 1720s with a Gothic spire atop a Greek-type temple, is an oasis of peace on busy Trafalgar Square. Though the interior is so-so, the venue is renowned for its concerts. Consider a free lunchtime concert (Mon, Tue, and Fri at 13:00), an evening concert (£9-28, several nights a week at 19:30), or Wednesday night jazz (£5.50-12, at 20:00). See the website for the full schedule. The church basement has a concert ticket office, gift shop, brass-rubbing center, and the recommended Café in the Crypt.

▶ *Free, but donations welcome. Hours vary but generally open Mon-Fri 8:30-13:00 & 14:00-18:00, Sat 9:30-18:00, Sun 15:30-17:00. Tube: Charing Cross. Tel. 020/7766-1100, www.stmartin-in-the-fields.org.*

The West End and Nearby

Once located "west" of the medieval walled city of London, this area is now London's liveliest. Theaters, pubs, restaurants, shopping, museums, and nightlife abound. ▲Leicester Square and ▲Piccadilly Circus form the nucleus of this area. To the north lie London's Chinatown, the theaters of Shaftesbury Avenue, and the trendy ▲Soho neighborhood. ▲▲Covent Garden—an arcade bristling with shops and colorful street life—is nearby, as are the shops of Regent Street. The best Tube stops are Leicester Square and Piccadilly.

✪ For more on all of the above sights, see the West End Walk chapter.

▲London Transport Museum

This modern, well-presented museum, located right at Covent Garden, is fun for kids and thought-provoking for adults. The growth of Europe's third-biggest city (after Istanbul and Moscow) has been made possible by its public transit system.

An elevator whisks you to the top floor...and the year 1800, when horse-drawn vehicles ruled the road. London invented the notion of a public bus traveling a set route that anyone could board without a reservation. Next came steam-powered locomotives speeding through tunnels beneath the city—the world's first underground Metro system (c. 1865). On the ground floor, horses and trains are quickly replaced by cars, taxis, red double-decker buses, streetcars, and 20th-century congestion. How to deal with it? Interactive exhibits let you be part of the solution.

▶ *£17. Open Sat-Thu 10:00-18:00, Fri 11:00-18:00, last entry 45 minutes before closing. There's a pleasant upstairs café with Covent Garden*

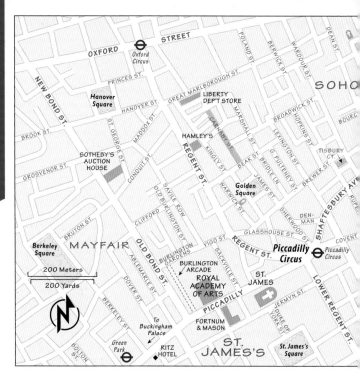

view. Tube: Covent Garden. Tel. 020/7379-6344, recorded info tel. 020/7565-7299, www.ltmuseum.co.uk.

▲Courtauld Gallery

Though it may be closed for renovation when you visit, if it is open, this gallery of paintings is just small enough that you could see it all in a single visit. The collection spans the history of Western painting, from medieval altarpieces through Italian Renaissance to the 20th century. Its highlights are Impressionist and Post-Impressionist works, some of which you'll recognize.

Be sure to see Edouard Manet's *A Bar at the Folies-Bergère,* which places you in the center of a glittering dancehall, reflected in the bar mirror.

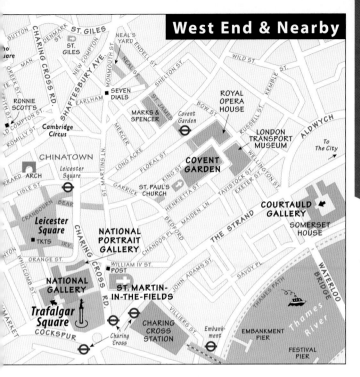

Paul Cézanne foreshadows Cubism with a mountain landscape built out of cubes of paint.

There's also Vincent van Gogh's *Self-Portrait with Bandaged Ear*, painted in the aftermath of the insane episode where he threatened Gauguin with a knife, cut off a piece of his own ear, and gave it to a prostitute. Just released from the hospital, Van Gogh assesses himself. The self-portrait shows a calm man with an unflinching gaze. The slightly stained bandage over his ear is neither hidden in shame nor worn as a badge of honor. Doesn't this man realize that a year and a half later he'll take his own life?

▶ *£7, price can change depending on exhibit. Open daily 10:00-18:00, sometimes open Thu until 21:00. Located at Somerset House, along the*

Strand, a 15-minute walk from Trafalgar (Tube: Temple or Covent Garden). There's a downstairs $$ cafeteria, plus other eateries around the complex. Recorded info tel. 020/7848-2526, shop tel. 020/7848-2579, www.courtauld.ac.uk.

Buckingham Palace

Buckingham Palace has been the official residence of the monarch since 1837, when Queen Victoria moved in. Today, Queen Elizabeth II and Prince Philip live here most of the time (in the north wing), though they have other residences elsewhere. When the Queen's at home, the royal standard flies (a red, yellow, and blue flag); otherwise, the Union Jack flaps in the wind. The palace is a cozy little 830,000-square-foot pad, home to a concert hall (for command performances), ballrooms for state functions, and the large enclosed gardens in back. As the place where foreign leaders are received, it's become the symbol of the monarchy.

The area around the palace is mostly open space and gardens, with few tourist amenities. The wide boulevard called The Mall was built in 1911 as a ceremonial approach.

For tourists, there are several sights to see: the Changing of the Guard out front, the Queen's Gallery art collection in a palace annex, and the stables of the adjoining Royal Mews. The Palace's main interior is off-limits to tourists except for the State Rooms visits in August and September (Tube: Victoria, St. James's Park, or Green Park).

▲▲Changing of the Guard at Buckingham Palace

This is the spectacle every visitor to London must see at least once: stone-faced, red-coated (or in winter, gray-coated), bearskin-hatted guards

Buckingham Palace—the Queen's humble home

Changing of the Guard—maximum pageantry

Buckingham Palace Area

ST. JAMES'S PALACE ❹

THE MALL

CLARENCE HOUSE

St. James's Park

LANCASTER HOUSE

Lake

To Hyde Park corner ←

Green Park

VICTORIA MEMORIAL

❷

CONSTITUTION HILL

Park

Private Park

BUCKINGHAM PALACE

❶

❺

SPUR RD.

BIRDCAGE WALK

GUARDS' CHAPEL

To Big Ben & Churchill War Rooms

QUEEN'S GALLERY

BUCKINGHAM PALACE ROAD

BUCKINGHAM GATE

Parade Ground

❸

WELLINGTON BARRACKS

GUARDS' MUSEUM

PETTY FRANCE

St. James's Park

ROYAL MEWS

GROSVENOR PL.
To Victoria Station ↙

❶ Changing of the Guard
❷ Victoria Memorial (Best Views)
❸ Wellington Barracks
❹ St. James's Palace
❺ Spur Road

Sights

changing posts with much fanfare, in an hour-long ceremony accompanied by a brass band. The most famous part takes place right in front of Buckingham Palace at 11:00. But there actually are several different guard-changing ceremonies and parades going on simultaneously, at different locations within a few hundred yards of the palace.

The main event (really a nonevent) is in the forecourt right in front of Buckingham Palace (between the palace and the fence) from 11:00 to 11:30. You'll need to get here as close to 10:00 as possible to get a place front and center, next to the fence. The key to good viewing is to get either right up front along the road or fence, or find a raised surface to stand or sit on—a balustrade or a curb—so you can see over people's heads.

The high ground on the circular Victoria Memorial provides the best overall view (come before 10:30 to get a place). From a high spot on the memorial, you have good (if more distant) views of the palace as well as the arriving and departing parades along The Mall and Spur Road.

If you don't feel like jostling for a view, stroll down to St. James's Palace and wait near the corner for a great photo-op. At about 11:45, the parade marches up The Mall to the palace and performs a smaller changing ceremony—with almost no crowds. Afterward, stroll through nearby St. James's Park.

Or to follow the procession, start in the courtyard of St. James's Palace (10:30) where the "Old Guard" mobilizes. Just before they leave (at 10:43), march ahead down Marlborough Street to The Mall. Pause here to watch them parade past, then cut through the park to the Wellington Barracks—where the "New Guard" is getting ready to leave for Buckingham (10:57). March along with the band and guards to the palace. At 11:00 the two groups meet in the courtyard, the band plays a few songs, and soldiers parade and finally exchange compliments before returning to Wellington Barracks and St. James's Palace (11:40).

▶ *Free. May-July daily at 11:00, every other day Aug-April, no ceremony in very wet weather, exact schedule subject to change—call 020/7766-7300 for the day's plan, or check www.householddivision.org.uk (search "Changing the Guard"); Tube: Victoria, St. James's Park, or Green Park. Or hop into a big black taxi and say, "Buck House, please." Tel. 020/7766-7300, www.royal.gov.uk.*

Other Buckingham Palace Sights

▲**State Rooms at Buckingham Palace:** The palace interior is off-limits to visitors, except during August and September, when you can pay to go inside and enjoy several lavish rooms, including the throne room.

▶ *£21.50, includes audioguide. Open Aug-Sept only, daily 9:30-18:30, last entry 17:15 in Aug, 16:15 in Sept. It's crowded—come by 9:00 or book ahead at tel. 0303/123-7300.*

▲**Queen's Gallery:** Queen Elizabeth's personal collection of world-class art is on display in a wing adjoining the palace. Small, thoughtfully presented, and always exquisite displays fill the five rooms open to the public. You'll also see temporary exhibits and a small room glittering with the Queen's personal jewelry. Men shouldn't miss the mahogany-trimmed urinals.

▶ *£10.30 but can change depending on exhibit. Open daily 10:00-17:30, from 9:30 Aug-Sept, last entry one hour before closing. Tel. 0303/123-7301, royalcollection.org.uk.*

A Page of History

The Beginnings: In 55 B.C., Julius Caesar invaded, and "Londinium" became a river-trade town and the hub of Britain. As Rome fell (A.D. 410), London was attacked by Saxons and Vikings. In 1066 the Normans invaded and built the Tower of London. As the city grew— London Bridge, Old St. Paul's—it became clear to wannabe kings that whoever controlled London controlled Britain. Monarchs built their palaces west of the city walls, near Westminster Abbey.

1500s: Charismatic Henry VIII thrust England onto the world stage, and London's population swelled to 50,000. His daughter, Elizabeth I, reigned over a cultural renaissance of sea exploration, scientific discovery, literature (Shakespeare), and fine manners.

1600s: Just when things were going so well, the Great Plague (1665) and Great Fire (1666) devastated the wooden city. London rebuilt—Christopher Wren designed St. Paul's and dozens of other churches—but the center of gravity had shifted to the West End.

1700s: Britannia ruled the waves, and London (pop. 500,000) bloomed with Georgian architecture, theater, daily newspapers, and the sounds of Handel's *Messiah*. When Admiral Nelson defeated Napoleon at sea, and the Duke of Wellington finished him off at Waterloo, Britain emerged as the world's No. 1 power.

1800s: Britain under Queen Victoria reigned supreme, steaming into the modern age with railroads, factories, telephones, and the first Underground. Meanwhile, Charles Dickens chronicled the darker elements, and Jack the Ripper prowled the soot-stained tenements.

20th Century: Two world wars whittled Britain down from an empire to a struggling nation. During World War II, the Nazi "Blitz" bombing campaign leveled eastern London. Britain's colonies demanded independence, and London was flooded with immigrants.

In the 1960s, "Swinging London" was a center for rock music (the Beatles, the Stones, the Who), fashion, and Austin Powers-style joie de vivre. The 1970s brought massive unemployment. The 1980s brought a conservative reaction and worldwide attention on Princess Diana.

21st Century: London is again one of the world's greatest cities, a hub of banking, art, technology, pop music, TV, and film.

Royal Mews: These are the palace's working stables. You'll see a few of the Queen's 30 horses, a fancy car, and a bunch of old carriages, finishing with the Gold State Coach (c. 1760, 4 tons, 4 mph).

▶ *£9.30. Open April-Oct daily 10:00-17:00; Nov-March Mon-Sat 10:00-16:00, closed Sun; last entry 45 minutes before closing. Located along Buckingham Palace Road. Tel. 0303/123-7302.*

NORTH LONDON

▲▲▲British Museum

As home to artifacts through the ages, a visit here is like taking a long hike through *Encyclopedia Britannica* National Park.

✪ See the British Museum Tour chapter.

▲▲▲British Library

A manageable collection of the literary treasures of Western civilization, from early Bibles to the Magna Carta to Shakespeare's *Hamlet* to Beatles lyrics.

✪ See the British Library Tour chapter.

▲Wallace Collection

Sir Richard Wallace's fine collection of 17th-century Dutch Masters, 18th-century French Rococo, medieval armor, and aristocratic fancies fills a sumptuous mansion. Paintings include *The Laughing Cavalier* by Frans Hals (as you walk by, his smirking eyes follow you) and *The Swing* by Jean-Honoré Fragonard (featuring an oblivious husband, a lurking lover, and a swinging wife).

Wallace Collection—aristocratic art

Madame Tussauds—Fab Four and more, in wax

▶ *Free, £5 suggested donation. Open daily 10:00-17:00, guided tours or lectures almost daily—call or check online to confirm times. Tube: Bond Street. Tel. 020/7563-9500, www.wallacecollection.org.*

▲Madame Tussauds Waxworks

This waxtravaganza is gimmicky and expensive, but dang good...a hit with the kind of travelers who skip the British Museum.

The original Madame Tussaud did wax casts of heads lopped off during the French Revolution (such as Marie-Antoinette's). She took her show on the road and ended up in London in 1835. These days, it's all about squeezing Leonardo DiCaprio's bum, singing with Lady Gaga, and partying with the Beatles, Benedict Cumberbatch, and Beyoncé. The place is one giant, crowded, chaotic photo-op, with everyone jockeying for position to pose next to some famous dummy. They're eerily realistic. Count how many times you say "excuse me" after bumping into a wax figure.

Sights that Stay Open Late

Most sightseeing in London winds up by 18:00, but there are several exceptions. Keep in mind that many of these sights stop admitting visitors well before their posted closing times.

Westminster Abbey (main church only): Wed until 19:00

Houses of Parliament: House of Commons—Oct-late July Mon until 22:30, Tue-Wed until 19:30; House of Lords—Oct-late July Mon-Wed until 22:00, Thu until 19:30

London Eye: Last ascent daily at 20:30, at 21:30 or later July-Aug

Madame Tussauds: July-Aug daily until 19:30 (last entry time; stays open about 2 hours later)

Clink Prison Museum: July-Sept daily until 21:00, Oct-June Sat-Sun until 19:30

British Museum (some galleries): Fri until 20:30

British Library: Tue-Thu until 20:00

National Gallery: Fri until 21:00

National Portrait Gallery: Thu-Fri until 21:00

Tate Modern: Fri-Sat until 22:00

Victoria and Albert Museum (some galleries): Fri until 22:00

Besides the lineup of A-list stars, you'll see sports heroes (Muhammad Ali), scientists (Einstein), artists (Van Gogh), writers (Shakespeare), and politicians (Barack Obama). You can pose with the Queen, Will, or Kate...or settle for Charles. Other gimmicky attractions (haunted house, 3-D movie) please the kids. The lineup of dummies changes often, depending on who's hot.

▶ £34. Open Mon-Fri 9:30-19:30, Sat-Sun 9:00-18:00, July-Aug and school holidays daily 8:30-19:30, last entry two hours before closing. Located at Marylebone Road, Tube: Baker Street.

To avoid the line, buy a Priority Entrance ticket on their website or a Fast Track ticket in advance (✿ see page 200). Check the website for discounts. Toll tel. 0871-894-3000, www.madametussauds.com.

Sir John Soane's Museum

Architects and fans of eclectic knickknacks love this quirky place, as do fans of interior decor. Tour this furnished townhouse on a bird-chirping square and see 19th-century chairs, lamps, and carpets, wood-paneled nooks and crannies, stained-glass skylights, and Soane's collection of ancient relics and curios. His famous paintings include Hogarth's series on *The Rake's Progress* (read the fun plot) and several excellent Canalettos. In 1833, just before his death, Soane established his house as a museum, stipulating that it be kept in the state he left it. You'll leave wishing you'd known the man.

▸ *Free, but donations appreciated. Open Tue-Sat 10:00-17:00, candlelit on first Tue of the month 18:00-21:00 (and open to first 250 people only), closed Sun-Mon. Long entry lines on Sat and first Tue. Located at 13 Lincoln's Inn Fields, a quarter-mile southeast of British Museum, Tube: Holborn. Tel. 020/7405-2107, www.soane.org.*

Abbey Road—Beatles Photo-Op

London is surprisingly devoid of sights associated with the famous '60s rock band. For a photo-op, go to Abbey Road and walk the famous crosswalk pictured on the *Abbey Road* album cover. From the St. John's Wood Tube station (with a Beatles info kiosk), it's a five-minute walk west down Grove End Road to the intersection with Abbey Road. The Abbey Road recording studio where the Beatles often recorded is the low-key, white building to the right of Abbey House. It's still a working studio, so you can't go inside. Ponder the graffiti on the low wall outside, and...imagine. To re-create the famous cover photo, shoot the crosswalk from the roundabout as you face north up Abbey Road. Shoes are optional.

THE CITY

In Shakespeare's day, London consisted of a one-square-mile area surrounding St. Paul's. Today, that square mile—the neighborhood known as "The City"—is still the financial heart of London, densely packed with history and bustling with business. The City stretches from Temple Church (near Blackfriars Bridge) to the Tower of London. Its spine is a single east-west street that changes names—the Strand becomes Fleet Street, then Cannon Street.

This was the London of the ancient Romans, William the Conqueror, Henry VIII, Shakespeare, and Elizabeth I. But The City has been stripped of its history by the Great Fire (1666), the WWII Blitz (1940-1941), and

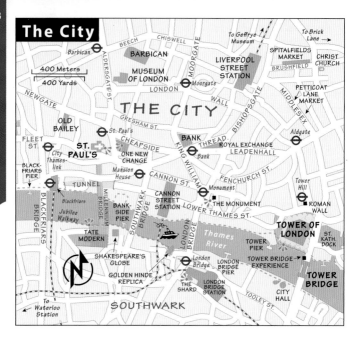

The City

To Geffrye Museum

To Brick Lane →

BEECH CHISWELL

Barbican

BARBICAN

MOORGATE

SPITALFIELDS MARKET

CHRIST CHURCH

400 Meters

400 Yards

MUSEUM OF LONDON

LIVERPOOL STREET STATION

BRUSHFIELD

ALDERSGATE ST.

LONDON

Moorgate

PETTICOAT LANE MARKET

NEWGATE

MIDDLESEX

WALL

THE CITY

BISHOPSGATE

OLD BAILEY

GRESHAM ST.

St. Paul's

CHEAPSIDE

BANK

THREAD

Aldgate

FLEET ST.

ST. PAUL'S

ONE NEW CHANGE

City Thameslink

ROYAL EXCHANGE

LEADENHALL

KING WILLIAM ST.

BLACK-FRIARS PIER

Mansion House

CANNON ST.

FENCHURCH ST.

Tower Hill

TUNNEL

Bank

ROMAN WALL

CANNON STREET STATION

THE MONUMENT

LOWER THAMES ST.

Monument

BLACKFRIARS BRIDGE

Blackfriars

MILLENNIUM BRIDGE

BANK-SIDE PIER

Jubilee Walkway

SOUTHWARK BRIDGE

TOWER OF LONDON

ST. KATH. DOCK

TATE MODERN

Thames River

TOWER PIER

SHAKESPEARE'S GLOBE

LONDON BRIDGE

London Bridge

LONDON BRIDGE PIER

TOWER BRIDGE EXPERIENCE

TOWER BRIDGE

GOLDEN HINDE REPLICA

N

THE SHARD

LONDON BRIDGE STATION

TOOLEY ST.

CITY HALL

To Waterloo Station

SOUTHWARK

modern economic realities. Today, it's a neighborhood of modern bank buildings and retail stores. Only about 10,000 people actually live here, but on work days it's packed with about 400,000 commuting bankers, legal assistants, and coffee-shop baristas. By day, The City is a hive of business activity. At night and on weekends, it's a ghost town. You can download a free 🎧 Rick Steves audio tour to accompany a stroll through The City (🟢 see page 201).

▲▲▲St. Paul's Cathedral

There's been a church here since 604. When Old St. Paul's Cathedral was incinerated in the Great Fire of 1666, Sir Christopher Wren (1632-1723) was hired to build a new and bigger church on the spot. Even now, as sky-scrapers encroach, Wren's 365-foot-high dome rises majestically above the rooftops of the neighborhood. St. Paul's is England's national church, and was the symbol of the city's survival of the Blitz of 1940. During "the Blitz"—when Nazi warplanes pummeled a defenseless London—St. Paul's was hit with 28 bombs. The surrounding neighborhood was absolutely flattened, but the church rose above it, seemingly miraculously, giving hope to London in its darkest hour. Today, St. Paul's is the nucleus of the Earth's 70 million Anglicans, a living war memorial, and the final resting place of many great Londoners. You can climb the dome for expansive views.

The spacious nave, at 515 feet long and 250 feet wide, is Europe's fourth largest. Stroll up the nave—the same one Prince Charles and Lady Diana walked on their 1981 wedding day. When you reach the base of the soaring, 65,000-ton dome, stand and gasp upward. The dome you see is only the innermost of Wren's ingenious three-in-one design. The second dome is visible when you look up through the opening at the top to see the light-filled lantern. Finally, the whole thing is covered on the outside by a third and final dome—the shell of lead-covered wood that you see from the street.

Wren's creation has the clean lines and geometric simplicity of the age of Newton, when reason was holy and God set the planets spinning in perfect geometrical motion. For more than 40 years, Wren worked on this site, overseeing every detail. At age 75, he got to look up and see his son place a cross on top of the dome, completing the masterpiece. On the floor directly beneath the dome is a brass grate with Wren's name and epitaph: *Lector, si monumentum requiris circumspice*—"Reader, if you seek his monument, look around you."

In the north transept, find the big painting *The Light of the World* (1904), by William Holman Hunt. In the dark of night, Jesus—with a lantern, halo, jeweled cape, and crown of thorns—approaches an out-of-the-way

St. Paul's, with Wren's 365-foot dome

Nelson lies directly beneath the dome.

home in the woods, knocks on the door, and listens for an invitation to come in. The painting is one of the world's best-known, but critics have always savaged it. A recent list of "Britain's Ten Worst Paintings" honored it as number seven.

Approaching the altar, you'll pass the abstract statue *Mother and Child* by Britain's greatest modern sculptor, Henry Moore, who was inspired by the sight of British moms nursing babies in WWII bomb shelters. Behind the altar is the American Memorial Chapel. The 500-page Roll of Honor lists the 28,000 Yanks based in Britain who sacrificed their lives to save Britain during World War II. The stained-glass windows even feature American iconography amid the saints. Spot the American eagle (center window, to the left of Christ), George Washington (right window, upper-right corner), and symbols of all 50 states.

Continuing on, you'll pass a shrouded statue of John Donne, the well-known poet ("No man is an island…"), who was also a passionate preacher in old St. Paul's (1621-1631).

To climb the dome, it's 528 steps to the top—no elevator. The tower has three levels, called galleries. The climb gets steeper, narrower, and more claustrophobic as you go higher. You don't have to do all three levels, but once you start to the next level, you can't turn back. After the initial 257 steps, you first reach the Whispering Gallery, with nice views of the church interior. The dome is constructed with such acoustic precision that sweet nothings whispered from one side of the dome can (supposedly) be heard on the opposite side, 170 feet away. After another set of stairs, you're at the Stone Gallery, offering expansive outdoor views of London. Finally, a long, tight staircase takes you to the top of the cupola, the Golden Gallery, with stunning views of the entire city.

You can also descend to the church crypt, where many famous people are buried (use the free church map to locate them), including Horatio Nelson (who wore down Napoleon) and the Duke of Wellington (who finished Napoleon off). The tomb of Christopher Wren—the man who built this glorious cathedral—is buried off in a corner in a humble grave marked with just a plain black slab.

▶ *£18 (£16 if purchased online in advance), includes dome climb. Open Mon-Sat 8:30-16:30 (dome opens at 9:30), closed Sun except for worship. It's wise to check online to confirm opening hours and worship times. Evensong (free) is Tue-Sat 17:00 and Sun 15:15 (but no sightseeing allowed). Guided tours (4/day) and audioguides are both included in*

Harry Potter's story is set in a magical Britain, and the places mentioned in the books are fictional, but you can visit many real (if unmagical) film locations.

Harry first realizes his wizard powers when talking with a boa constrictor, filmed at the **London Zoo's Reptile House** in Regent's Park (Tube: Great Portland Street). **Big Ben** and **Parliament,** along the Thames, welcome Harry to the modern city inhabited by non-magical Muggles. Harry shops with Hagrid in glass-roofed **Leadenhall Market** (Tube: Bank) along Bull's Head Passage. Goblin-run Gringotts Wizarding Bank was filmed in the chandeliered entryway of **Australia House** (Tube: Temple).

Harry catches the train to Hogwarts at **King's Cross/St. Pancras Station,** departing from magical **platform 9¾** (where the station has placed a sign and disappearing luggage cart near real platform 9—and a Harry Potter gift shop). In the **Prisoner of Azkaban** film, Harry careens through the city on a three-decker bus that dumps him off at the southeast edge of **Borough Market** (Tube: London Bridge). In the **Half-Blood Prince** film, the **Millennium Bridge** collapses into the Thames. For the **Deathly Hallows** films, the real government offices of **Whitehall** serve as the location for the Ministry of Magic.

Other London settings, like Diagon Alley, only exist at **Leavesden Film Studios** (20 miles north of London), where most of the films' interiors were shot. Here, Harry Potter pilgrims can see many of the original sets and props on the Warner Bros. Studio Tour (£35, kids £27). Tours generally depart daily 9:00-18:30, but times can vary. Visiting Leavesden takes most of a day (tel. 0845-084-0900, www.wbstudiotour. co.uk). You can get there via train from Euston Station or via a pricey-but-convenient Golden Tours bus from near Victoria Station (www. goldentours.com).

---

admission, or you can 🎧 *download a free Rick Steves audio tour (✪ see page 201). No photos. Good $ café in the crypt, and helpful TI across the street. Located at Tube: St. Paul's, or by handy buses #15 and #11 (✪ see page 196). Recorded info tel. 020/7246-8348, reception tel. 020/7246-8350, www.stpauls.co.uk.*

▲Old Bailey

England's most infamous criminals—from the king-killers of the Civil War to the radically religious William Penn, from the "criminally homosexual" Oscar Wilde to the Yorkshire Ripper—were tried here, in Britain's highest criminal court. Today, they still dole out justice the old-fashioned way. Bewigged barristers argue before stern judges while the accused sits in the dock. It's open to the public when court is in session.

▶ *Free. Open generally Mon-Fri 10:00-13:00 & 14:00-17:00, closed Sat-Sun. Tight security—check bags at Capable Travel Agency, just down the street at Old Bailey 4—£5/bag, £1 per phone or camera. Located on Old Bailey Street, follow signs to visitor's entrance, Tube: St. Paul's. Tel. 020/7248-3277, www.cityoflondon.gov.uk.*

▲Museum of London

Trace the fascinating story of London's distinguished citizens, from Neanderthals to Romans to Elizabethans to Victorians to Mods to today. The museum's displays are chronological, spacious, and informative without being overwhelming. Scale models and costumes help you visualize everyday life in the city at different periods. There are enough whiz-bang multimedia displays (including the Plague and the Great Fire) to spice up otherwise humdrum artifacts. This regular stop for the local school kids gives the best overview of London history in town.

▶ *Free, daily 10:00-18:00, last entry one hour before closing, see the day's events board for special talks and tours, café, on London Wall at Aldersgate Street, Tube: Barbican or St. Paul's plus 5-minute walk. Tel. 020/7001-9844, www.museumoflondon.org.uk.*

The Monument to the Great Fire

The 202-foot column known as The Monument, built by Christopher Wren, commemorates the Great Fire that transformed London. At 2:00 in the morning of September 2, 1666, a small fire broke out in a baker's oven in nearby Pudding Lane. Fanned by hot, blustery weather, the fire swept westward, leaping from house to house. It engulfed the mostly wooden city, devouring Old St. Paul's, and continuing to Temple Church, until The City was a square mile of flame. In four days, 80 percent of London was incinerated, including 13,000 houses and 89 churches. The good news? Incredibly, only nine people died, the fire cleansed a plague-infested city, and Wren was around to rebuild London's skyline. You can climb The Monument's 311 steps for a view that's still pretty monumental.

▸ *£4 (£11 combo-ticket with Tower Bridge, cash only), daily 9:30-18:00, until 17:30 Oct-March. Located at the northeast end of London Bridge, Tube: Monument. Tel. 020/7626-2717, www.themonument.info.*

▲▲▲Tower of London

This vast castle complex stars the crown jewels, witty Beefeater tours, and the executioner's site that dispensed with a couple of Henry VIII's wives. ✪ See the Tower of London Tour chapter.

Tower Bridge

The iconic Tower Bridge—often mistakenly called London Bridge—was built in 1894 as a hydraulically powered drawbridge to accommodate the growing East End. You can tour the bridge and its workings at the Tower Bridge Exhibition.

▸ *£9 (£11 combo-ticket with Monument, credit cards accepted), daily 10:00-18:00 in summer, 9:30-17:30 in winter. Tube: Tower Hill. Tel. 020/7403-3761, www.towerbridge.org.uk.*

THE SOUTH BANK

South of the Thames is a thriving area tied together by a riverside pedestrian path called the Jubilee Walkway. Stretching from the London Eye to London Bridge, it offers grand views of the city skyline across the river. On a sunny day, this is the place to see London out strolling.

The area hosts major sights—Shakespeare's Globe, the Tate Modern—plus some tacky ones, all spiced with pleasant pubs, theaters, and cafes. Several Thames cruise boats stop along the South Bank (✪ see page 206). Helpful Tube stops are Waterloo, Southwark, and London Bridge.

▲▲London Eye

The giant Ferris wheel, towering above London opposite Big Ben, is London's answer to the Eiffel Tower. While the experience is memorable, London doesn't have much of a skyline to see, and the price is borderline outrageous.

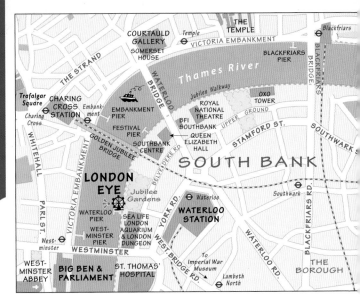

Twenty-five people ride in each of its 32 air-conditioned capsules for the 30-minute rotation (you go around only once). From the top of this 443-foot-high wheel—the second-highest public viewpoint in the city, with 25 miles' visibility on the rare clear day—even Big Ben looks small. While it was originally built to celebrate the new millennium, the Eye is now a permanent fixture of the London skyline.

Your ticket also includes a bombastic-but-fun, four-minute, 3-D movie. By the Eye there's a cotton-candy tourist zone of kitschy, kid-friendly attractions, as well as Thames cruise boats.

▶ £24.95, combo-tickets available with other attractions. Open daily 10:00-20:30, until 21:30 or later in July and August, check website for latest schedule, closed Dec 25 and a few days in Jan. Tube: Waterloo or Westminster.

Expect 30-minute waits to buy tickets, plus 30-45-minute waits to board, especially weekends from 11:00-17:00, and every day July-Aug. An £8 Fast Track supplement lets you walk straight on. Avoid the

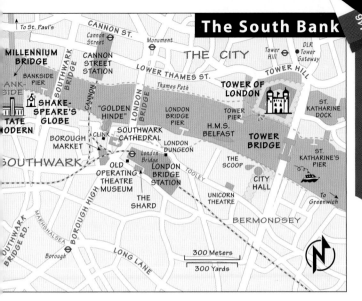

In the map:

To St. Paul's

CANNON ST.

Cannon Street

Monument

THE CITY

Tower Hill

DLR
Tower Gateway

MILLENNIUM BRIDGE

CANNON STREET STATION

LOWER THAMES ST.

TOWER HILL

BANKSIDE PIER

ANK-SIDE

SHAKE-SPEARE'S GLOBE

TATE MODERN

"GOLDEN HINDE"

Thames Path

TOWER OF LONDON

ST. KATHARINE DOCK

CLINK

SOUTHWARK CATHEDRAL

LONDON BRIDGE PIER

TOWER PIER

H.M.S. BELFAST

BOROUGH MARKET

LONDON DUNGEON

TOWER BRIDGE

ST. KATHARINE'S PIER

SOUTHWARK

OLD OPERATING THEATRE MUSEUM

London Bridge

LONDON BRIDGE STATION

THE SCOOP

CITY HALL

To Greenwich

THE SHARD

TOOLEY

UNICORN THEATRE

SOUTHWARK BRIDGE RD.

MARSHALSEA

BOROUGH HIGH ST.

BERMONDSEY

Borough

LONG LANE

300 Meters

300 Yards

N

ticket-buying part of the wait by booking online (10 percent discount) or by phone. Tel. 0870-500-0600, www.londoneye.com.

▲▲Imperial War Museum

This impressive, engrossing museum covers the wars of the 20th and 21st centuries with lots of artifacts and video clips. War wonks love the place, as do history buffs who enjoy patiently reading displays. For the rest, there are enough interactive experiences and multimedia exhibits and submarines for the kids to climb in to keep it interesting.

Highlights include the World War I galleries, which were renovated for the war's 100-year anniversary, and the World War II rooms, which are augmented by the Blitz Experience, a walk-through simulator that assaults the senses with the noise and intensity of a Nazi air raid.

You'll see vintage planes, tanks, submarines, and a 50-foot V-2 rocket, the kind Hitler rained down on London. The section on the "Secret War" peeks into the intrigues of espionage. The Holocaust exhibit is one of the

The high-caliber Imperial War Museum   Tate Modern—powerhouse art in a powerhouse

best on the subject anywhere. The displays continue through the Cold War, the Cuban Missile Crisis, the Troubles in Northern Ireland, the wars in Iraq and Afghanistan, and terrorism. Rather than glorify war, the museum shines a light on the 100 million deaths of the 20th century—the tragic consequence of one of humankind's most persistent traits.

▸ *Free, £5 suggested donation, temporary exhibits extra. Open daily 10:00-18:00. Tube: Lambeth North. Tel. 020/7416-5000, www.iwm.org.uk.*

▲▲Tate Modern

Dedicated in the spring of 2000, the striking museum across the river from St. Paul's opened the new century with art from the previous one. Its powerhouse collection of Monet, Matisse, Dalí, Picasso, Warhol, and much more is displayed in a converted powerhouse.

The permanent collection is on the third and fifth floors. Paintings are arranged according to theme, not chronologically or by artist. Paintings by Picasso, for example, are scattered all over the building. Don't just come to see the Old Masters of modernism. Push your mental envelope with more recent works by Pollock, Miró, Bacon, Picabia, Beuys, Twombly, and others.

Of equal interest are the many temporary exhibits featuring cutting-edge art. A new annex provides even more display space. Each year, the main hall features a different monumental installation by a prominent artist—always one of the highlights of the art world.

▸ *Free, £4 donations appreciated, fee for special exhibitions. Open daily 10:00-18:00, Fri-Sat until 22:00—good times to visit. Free guided tours several times a day. $$$$ View restaurant on top floor. Located across* *the Millennium Bridge from St. Paul's. Tube: Southwark, London Bridge, or Mansion House. Tel. 020/7887-8888, www.tate.org.uk.*

▲Millennium Bridge

The pedestrian bridge linking St. Paul's Cathedral and the Tate Modern opened in the year 2000. Almost immediately, the $25 million "bridge to the next millennium" started wobbling dangerously (insert your own ironic joke here). Now stabilized, it's won praise for Sir Norman Foster's sleek minimalist design—370 yards long, four yards wide, of stainless steel with teak planks.

▲▲Shakespeare's Globe

> *All the world's a stage,*
> *And all the men and women merely players.*
> *They have their exits and their entrances,*
> *And one man, in his time, plays many parts.*
> —As You Like It

In 1599, 35-year-old William Shakespeare and his theater company opened the 3,000-seat Globe Theatre, by far the largest of its day. The Globe premiered Shakespeare's greatest works—*Hamlet, Othello, King Lear, Macbeth*—in open-air summer afternoon performances. In 1612, during a performance of *Henry VIII*, a stage cannon sparked a fire. Within an hour, the wood-and-thatch building had burned completely to the ground.

In 1997, this replica was built—round, half-timbered, and thatched—located a block from the original site. It's a working theater, hosting plays virtually every day May through September. Productions range from Shakespeare plays in period costumes to modern interpretations of his works and some works by other playwrights. As at the old Globe, the new one has an open-air roof, standing room by the stage, and no curtain. It's also more modern—with female actors, lights for night performances, a concrete floor, and fire-resistant materials. Today's Globe accommodates 800 seated and 600 standing versus Shakespeare's 2,200 seated and 1,000 groundlings. An indoor Jacobean theater at the complex hosts period plays and concerts year-round.

Besides attending plays, you can pay admission to tour the theater and a museum called the Exhibition. You first see the Exhibition, a museum

Shakespeare's Globe hosts plays (in summer) and lets visitors tour the theater and museum.

of Elizabethan-era memorabilia, including some early folios—the first publications of Shakespeare's plays. Then an energetic guide leads you into
the theater to see the stage and the different seating areas for the different
classes of people, bringing the Elizabethan period to life.

▶ *£15 includes museum and 40-minute tour. Complex open daily 9:00-
17:00, tours start every 30 minutes. During theater season (late April-
mid-Oct), when the theater closes for performances, the last tour is Mon
at 17:00, Tue-Sat at 12:30, Sun at 11:30; or you can visit the Exhibition
only (£6). The theater complex also has a box office and eateries, from
fancy to takeout. Located near the Tate Modern smokestack, Tube:
Mansion House or London Bridge. Tel. 020/7902-1400, box office tel.
020/7401-9919, www.shakespearesglobe.com.*

▲Southwark

The area between the Tate Modern and London Bridge is known as
Southwark (SUTH-uck). In Shakespeare's day, this was the rowdy neighborhood where Londoners went for a night of theater, bear-and-dog fights,
brothels, and rollicking pubs. Today it's been gentrified, and within a few

blocks (near Tube: London Bridge), you'll find several interesting (and some tacky) sights.

The Clink Prison Museum: This was, until 1780, where law-abiding citizens threw Southwark troublemakers. Today, it's a low-tech, tacky torture museum filling grotty old rooms with papier-mâché gore.

▶ *Overpriced at £7.50. Open July-Sept daily 10:00-21:00; Oct-June Mon-Fri 10:00-18:00, Sat-Sun until 19:30. Located at 1 Clink Street. Tel. 020/7403-0900, www.clink.co.uk.*

***Golden Hinde* Replica:** As we all learned in school, "Sir Francis Drake circumcised the globe with a hundred-foot clipper." Or something like that... This is a full-size, working replica of that 16th-century warship in which Drake circumnavigated the globe (1577-1580), becoming history's most successful pirate.

▶ *Free to view from outside, £6 to enter. Open daily 10:00-17:00. Tel. 020/7403-0123, www.goldenhinde.com.*

Southwark Cathedral: Highlights include a Shakespeare memorial (right wall), a chapel to university-founding John Harvard (left wall), and evensong services (Tue-Fri 17:30, Sat 16:00, Sun 15:00).

▶ *Free, £4 suggested donation. Open Mon-Fri 8:00-18:00, Sat-Sun 8:30-18:00. Tel. 020/7367-6700, http://cathedral.southwark.anglican.org.*

Borough Market: For over 800 years, there's been a produce market here. These days there are as many people taking photos as buying fruit, cheese, and beautiful breads, but it's still a fun carnival atmosphere with fantastic stall food. For maximum market and minimum crowds, join the locals on Thursdays (10:00-17:00). Located next to Southwark Cathedral, Tube: London Bridge; www.boroughmarket.org.uk.

London Bridge: Built in 1972, this is the unimpressive fourth incarnation of the famed 2,000-year-old river crossing. Farther east is the egg-shaped City Hall building and an outdoor amphitheater called The Scoop, which hosts free summer entertainment.

▲Old Operating Theatre Museum and Herb Garret

Climb a tight and creaky staircase to find a garret used to dry medicinal herbs, crude Victorian surgical instruments reminiscent of Black & Decker, and a special look at anesthetics—ether, chloroform, or three pints of ale.

Then you stumble upon Britain's oldest operating theater—a semi-circular room accommodating 150 spectators—where doctors sawed off limbs while med students observed. The wood still bears bloodstains.

Nearly one in three patients died. There was a fine line between Victorian-era surgeons and Jack the Ripper.

▶ *£6.50, cash only. Open daily 10:30-17:00. At 9a St. Thomas Street, Tube: London Bridge. Tel. 020/7188-2679, www.thegarret.org.uk.*

The Shard

Rocketing dramatically 1,020 feet above the south end of the London Bridge, this recent addition to London's skyline is the tallest building in Western Europe. Seventy floors up are observation decks with exceptional views (and ticket prices as high as the building itself).

▶ *£31, cheaper if booked online at least a day in advance. Open daily 10:00-22:00, last entry one hour before closing. Sunny weekends can be fully booked; it's least crowded on weekday mornings. Pretty good views even in bad weather. Tube: London Bridge—use London Bridge exit. Tel. 0844-499-7111, www.theviewfromtheshard.com.*

WEST LONDON

▲▲Tate Britain

Tate Britain specializes in British painting from the 16th century through modern times. This is people's art, with realistic paintings rooted in the people, landscape, and stories of the British Isles. You'll see Hogarth's sketches of gritty London life, Gainsborough's twinkle-toe ladies, Blake's glowing angels, Constable's clouds, the swooning realism of the Pre-Raphaelites, and room after room of Turner's proto-Impressionist tempests. In the modern art wing, there are Francis Bacon's screaming nightmares, Henry Moore statues, and the camera-eye portraits of Hockney and Freud.

Even if these names are new to you, don't worry. You'll likely see a few "famous" works you didn't know were British and exit the Tate Britain with at least one new favorite artist.

▶ *Free, £4 suggested donation, optional special exhibits extra. Open daily 10:00-18:00, last entry 45 minutes before closing. Free tours generally daily. $ Café and $$$$ restaurant. Located at Tube: Pimlico. Tel. 020/7887-8888, www.tate.org.uk.*

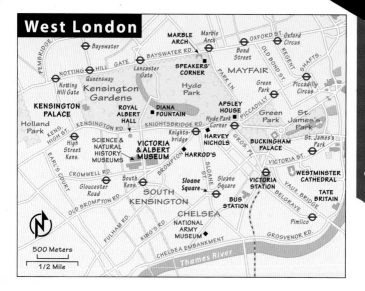

▲Apsley House (Wellington Museum)

Having beaten Napoleon at Waterloo, Arthur Wellesley, the First Duke of Wellington, was given a huge fortune with which he purchased London's ultimate address, #1 London. His mansion offers a nice interior, a few world-class paintings, and a glimpse at the life of the great soldier and two-time prime minister.

An 11-foot statue of Napoleon greets you. The two great men were polar opposites—Napoleon the daring general and champion of revolution, Wellington the play-it-safe strategist and conservative politician—but they're forever linked in history. You'll see precious objects given by the crowned heads of Europe, who were eternally grateful to Wellington for saving their necks from the guillotine. Among the wall-to-wall paintings are Van Dyck's *Charles I on Horseback* and works by Velázquez, Jan Steen, and Goya. There's also a pair of Wellington's boots, which the duke popularized—Brits today still call rubber boots "wellies."

▶ £9.70. Open Wed-Sun 11:00-17:00, closed Mon-Tue. Tube: Hyde Park Corner. Tel. 020/7499-5676, www.english-heritage.org.uk.

Tate Britain—art with deep British roots

Victoria and Albert—eclectic and surprising

▲Hyde Park and Speakers' Corner

London's "Central Park," originally Henry VIII's hunting grounds, has more than 600 acres of lush greenery. There's the huge manmade Serpentine Lake (with rental boats), the royal Kensington Palace, the ornate Albert Memorial across from the Royal Albert Hall, and (nearby) the Princess Diana Memorial Fountain. The western half of the park is known as Kensington Gardens. Plenty of bike-rental racks (use credit card) make getting around a breeze.

On Sunday afternoons, Speakers' Corner offers soapbox oratory at its best (northeast corner of the park, Tube: Marble Arch). Characters climb their stepladders, wave their flags, and emphatically share their views. "The grass roots of democracy" originated when the gallows stood here and the criminal was allowed to say just about anything before he swung. It's easy to raise your voice and gather a crowd—I dare you.

▲▲▲Victoria and Albert Museum

The world's top collection of decorative arts (vases, stained glass, fine furniture, clothing, jewelry, carpets, and more) is an eclectic and surprisingly interesting assortment. Throw in historical artifacts, a few masterpieces of painting and sculpture, and a bed that sleeps seven, and you have a museum built for browsing.

Here's just a sample: Five of Leonardo da Vinci's notebooks, underwear through the ages, a Chihuly chandelier, a life-size David with detachable fig leaf, Henry VIII's quill pen, and Mick Jagger's sequined jumpsuit. From the worlds of Islam and India, there are stunning carpets, the ring of the man who built the Taj Mahal, and a mechanical tiger that eats Brits. Best of all, the objects are all quite beautiful. You could spend days in the place. Pick up a museum map and wander at will.

▶ *Free, £5 donation requested, fees for special exhibits. Open daily 1ᵕ
17:45, some galleries open Fri until 22:00. Free tours daily. Tube: Sou▪
Kensington, from the Tube station a long tunnel leads directly to museum. Tel. 020/7942-2000, www.vam.ac.uk.*

▲▲Natural History Museum

Across the street from Victoria and Albert, this mammoth museum contains 50 million specimens of earth's treasures—living things in one half,
inanimate rocks and geology in the other. In the main hall, above a big di-
nosaur skeleton and under a massive slice of sequoia tree, Charles Darwin
sits as if upon a throne overseeing it all. Behind Darwin is the Treasures
Gallery displaying the museum's greatest hits: a dodo skeleton, a moon
rock, an extinct auk, etc.

Kids and non-science majors love the place. Well-explained and interactive exhibits cover dinosaurs, human evolution, creepy-crawlies, vol-
canoes, and more. Don't miss the meteorite from Mars and the Aurora
Pyramid of Hope, displaying 296 diamonds showing their full range of natural colors. Pop into the wild collection of dinosaurs if only to hear English
children exclaim, "Oh my goodness!"

▶ *Free, £5 donation requested, fees for optional special exhibits. Open
daily 10:00-18:00, open later last Fri of month. Free visitor app available
via the "Visit" section of the website. A long tunnel leads directly from
South Kensington Tube station to the museum. Tel. 020/7942-5011,
www.nhm.ac.uk.*

▲Science Museum

Next door to the Natural History Museum, this sprawling wonderland for
curious minds is kid-perfect, with themes such as measuring time, exploring space, and the evolution of modern medicine. It offers hands-on fun,
from moonwalks to deep-sea exploration, with trendy technology, always
interesting temporary exhibits, and an IMAX theater (£11).

▶ *Free, £5 suggested donation, open daily 10:00-18:00, until 19:00 during
school holidays, last entry 45 minutes before closing. Tube: South Kensington. Tel. 0870-870-4868, www.sciencemuseum.org.uk.*

▲▲Kensington Palace

For nearly 150 years (1689-1837), Kensington was the royal residence,
before Buckingham Palace became the official home of the monarch.

Sitting primly on its pleasant parkside grounds, the palace is immaculately restored. It gives a glimpse into the lives of several important residents, especially Queen Victoria, who was born and raised here. Today, Prince William, Duchess Kate, and little George and Charlotte call Kensington home, though—as many disappointed visitors discover—these more recent apartments are never open to the public.

From the central vestibule, signs direct you to the three main exhibits. The **Queen's State Apartments** focuses on the palace's first royal residents, William and Mary. In 1689, they moved into this Christopher Wren-built palace in what was then the peaceful village of Kensington. In the Big Hall, you get a sense of the grandeur of the palace—the dances and banquets held here, with expansive views over gardens landscaped in the Dutch style. Conceptual exhibits in successive rooms detail the problems that arose when the family failed to produce an heir.

The **King's State Apartments** are more lavishly decorated, giving the best look at court life during the palace's heyday in the 1700s—the salons attended by wits and intellectuals; the privy chamber, where Queen Caroline, wife of King George IV, once received Isaac Newton; the cupola room, where lords and ladies danced in ruffled sleeves and wide skirts; and the drawing room, for card games and politics. The king's gallery has world-class paintings by Tintoretto (*Esther Before Ahaserus*) and Veronese (*Adoration of the Kings*).

The **Victoria Revealed** exhibit traces the story of Queen Victoria's life, displayed in the very rooms where she grew up. You see the tiny dress the 4'11", 18-year-old monarch wore on her 1837 inauguration day, and the wedding dress from the marriage to her beloved Prince Albert. In the room where Victoria was born, there's her childhood doll collection and portraits of some of her own nine children. A room shrouded in dark evokes Albert's sudden and tragic death. Victoria would dress in black for the rest of her life. She lived to be 82, and you can watch film footage of her Diamond Jubilee celebration.

Outside the palace, garden enthusiasts enjoy the secluded Sunken Garden, and anyone can enjoy afternoon tea at the nearby Orangery.

▶ *£18. Open daily 10:00-18:00, Nov-Feb until 17:00, last entry one hour before closing, least crowded in mornings. It's a 10-minute stroll through Kensington Gardens from either Queensway or High Street Kensington Tube stations. Tel. 0844-482-7788, www.hrp.org.uk.*

GREATER LONDON

London's excellent public transit makes a number of outlying sights accessible. I've highlighted four of my favorites. Budget the better part of a sightseeing day to visit any of these. For three of the following sights, consider a Thames boat cruise as a scenic alternative to the train or Tube.

▲▲Kew Gardens

For a fine riverside park and a palatial greenhouse jungle to swing through, take the Tube or the boat to every botanist's favorite escape, Kew Gardens. Garden lovers could spend days here. Wander across 300 acres, among 33,000 different types of plants, representing the botanical diversity of our planet.

For a fragrant one-hour visit, concentrate on three buildings. The Palm House is a humid Victorian world of iron, glass, and tropical plants built in 1844. The Waterlily House has sights Monet would swim for. The Princess of Wales Conservatory is a modern greenhouse with many different climate zones growing countless cacti, bug-munching carnivorous plants, and more. The Xstrata Treetop Walkway, a 200-yard-long steel footbridge—puts you high in the canopy 60 feet above the ground. End your visit with a sun-dappled lunch or afternoon tea at the $$ Orangery.

▶ *£16.50 (June-Aug £11 after 16:00). Open April-Aug Mon-Fri 10:00-18:30, Sat-Sun 10:00-19:30, closes earlier Sept-March. Glasshouses close at 17:30 in high season, earlier off-season.*

Getting There: The Kew Gardens Tube station is two blocks from the main entrance. Boats run April-Oct from Westminster Pier—✪ see page 206. Tel. 020/8332-5000, recorded info 020/8332-5655, www.kew.org.

Kensington Palace—Will and Kate's home

Kew Gardens—tropical plants near London

Sights

▲▲Greenwich

Just downstream from London, Greenwich is the destination for all things salty, including the Cutty Sark clipper ship, the area's premier attraction (it's a good idea to reserve a ticket in advance and plan your day around your entry time). At the Royal Observatory, visitors pose for a photo-op along the prime meridian (0° longitude), straddling two hemispheres, while they set their watches to coordinate to Greenwich Mean Time, measured from here. Thanks to this time standard (and to seaworthy clocks that could be taken aboard ships), sailors could finally plot their east-west (longitudinal) location.

The National Maritime Museum holds everything from a giant working paddlewheel to the uniform Admiral Nelson wore when he was killed at Trafalgar (find the bullet hole). The town of Greenwich is a pleasant, manageable place for a riverside stroll, enjoying stunning Baroque architecture and open-air markets. Finish your stroll with lunch at the $$ Trafalgar Tavern, a pub Charles Dickens wrote about. Ahoy!

▶ *Most sights are open daily and many are free, but the town's popular market is closed Monday.*

Getting There: Boats depart from the piers at Westminster, Waterloo, and the Tower of London (2/hour, 30-75 minutes). By train, catch the DLR from Bank-Monument Tube station to Cutty Sark (20 minutes, 5/hour, covered by any Tube pass).

▲Hampton Court Palace

Fifteen miles up the Thames from downtown, and worth ▲▲ for palace aficionados, is the 500-year-old palace of Henry VIII. The stately Tudor palace overlooking the Thames was also home to Elizabeth I and Charles I. Visitors can see impressive Tudor rooms, including the King's apartments and a Great Hall with a magnificent hammer-beam ceiling. The industrial-strength Tudor kitchen kept 600 schmoozing courtiers thoroughly fed. The sculpted garden features a rare Tudor tennis court and a popular maze.

▶ *£21, online discounts. Open daily April-Oct 10:00-18:00, Nov-March until 16:30, last entry one hour before closing, café.*

Getting There: Train (2/hour, 35 minutes) from London's Waterloo Station, or taxi (£20) from Kew Gardens. The 3-4-hour boat ride from Westminster Pier (✪ see page 206) is relaxing and scenic. Tel. 0844-482-7777, www.hrp.org.uk.

▲Windsor

Queen Elizabeth II's preferred residence is Windsor Castle, set in the compact, pedestrian-friendly town of Windsor (pop. 30,000). Here you can see a low-key Changing of the Guard, the castle's lavish staterooms (perhaps Britain's best), an impressive royal art collection, some royal tombs, and Queen Mary's Dollhouse—a 1:12 scale palace in miniature.

▶ *Castle costs £20. To skip ticket lines, buy advance tickets online. Open daily March-Oct 9:30-17:15, Nov-Feb 9:45-16:15, last entry 1.25 hours before closing, may close for special events—call first, tel. 020/7766-7324, www.royalcollection.org.uk.*

Getting There: Trains run from both Paddington and Waterloo Stations (35-55 minutes, 2/hour, £10-22 round trip).

Sleeping

London is an expensive city for lodging. Cheaper rooms are relatively dumpy. I look for places that are clean, central, friendly, quiet, offer good value, and are small enough to have a hands-on owner and stable staff. Four of these six virtues means it's a keeper. Most of all, I emphasize location—all of my recommended accommodations are in safe, pleasant neighborhoods convenient to sightseeing.

The **Victoria Station** neighborhood (near Big Ben and Buckingham Palace) is central as can be. The area is safe, tidy, and full of decent eateries, and most hotels are a five-minute walk from Tube, bus, and train stations. **South Kensington** (west of Big Ben) is quiet, classy, and upscale, conveniently located on the Tube Circle Line. Residential **Notting Hill** (west of Hyde Park) is farther from the action, but it's also trendy and

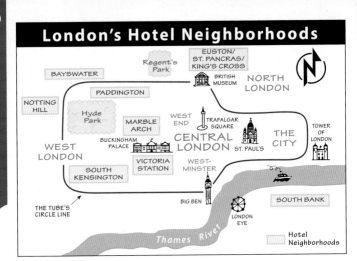

London's Hotel Neighborhoods

popular with the young international set. **Paddington Station** (north of Hyde Park) is less charming but has all the travelers' amenities and easy transportation connections.

You'll find convenient (if less charming) places near **Euston, St. Pancras, and King's Cross Stations.** The centrally located neighborhood **north of Marble Arch** is classy and close to Oxford Street shopping. Finally, for those wanting to stay south of the Thames near Shakespeare's Globe, there's the **South Bank.**

A Typical London Hotel Room

Double rooms listed in this book average around £100 (reasonably cheery, but small and old-fashioned by American standards). They range from around £80 (safe but cramped, with a bathroom down the hall) to £160 or more (spacious, elegant places with all the modern conveniences). Those on a tight budget may have to choose between a modern-but-soulless place, or family-run friendliness in a cracked-plaster building.

A £100 double room in London will be small and old-fashioned by American standards. It will have one double bed or two twins. There's a bathroom in the room with a toilet, sink, and shower. The room has a telephone, a TV, and often a plug-in kettle with free coffee and tea packets. At

Hotel Price Code

$$$$	**Splurge:** Most rooms are £160 or more
$$$	**Pricier:** £120–£160
$$	**Moderate:** £80–£120
$	**Budget:** £40–£80
¢	**Hostel/Backpacker:** Under £40
RS%	**Rick Steves discount**

These ranges cover rates for a standard double room during high season. Breakfast and 20 percent VAT tax are generally included in prices. For the best prices, book direct.

this price, the room probably does not have air-conditioning. The building has thin walls, several floors of rooms, steep stairs, and no elevator. Single rooms, triples, and quads will have similar features.

Breakfast is usually included in the price and consists of either a generous buffet (pastries, cereal, fruit, coffee) or a full English breakfast of bacon-and-eggs and more.

The hotel will have Internet access, either Wi-Fi or a public terminal in the lobby. At many of my listings, at least one of these options is free. The staff—which often includes recent immigrants—speaks enough English to get by.

Making Reservations

Reserve at least several weeks or even months in advance for peak season (June-Aug) or for a major holiday. Do it through the hotel's website, by phone, or with an email that reads something like this:

Dear Hotel Britannia,

I would like to reserve a double room for 2 people for 3 nights, arriving 19 July and departing 22 July. If possible, I would like a quiet room with a double bed (not twin beds), air-conditioning, and a bathroom inside the room. Please let me know if you have a room available and the price. Thank you.

Note that an "en suite" room has a bathroom in the room, while a "standard" room has the bathroom down the hall (though there's a sink in the room).

If the hotel requires your credit-card number for a deposit, you can send it by email (I do), but it's safer via phone, the hotel's secure website, or split between two emails. Once your room is booked, print out the confirmation, and reconfirm your reservation with a phone call or email a day or two in advance (alert them if you'll be arriving after 17:00). If canceling a reservation, some hotels require advance notice—otherwise they may bill you. Even if there's no penalty, it's polite to give at least three days' notice.

Budget Tips

To get the best deals, book directly with the hotel, not through a hotel-booking engine. Start with the hotel's website, looking for promo deals (official rates can drop 30 percent, especially at pricier hotels). Check rates every few days, as prices can change day to day depending on demand. Email several hotels to ask for their best price and compare offers. When you contact the hotel, you may get a cheaper rate if you offer to pay cash,

Looking for Hotel Deals Online

If small-hotel coziness is not your priority, you can often snag great online deals at high-rise, three- and four-star business hotels.

Big Hotel Chains: Try Millennium/Copthorne, Thistle, InterContinental/Holiday Inn, Radisson, Hilton, and Red Carnation.

Auction-type Sites: Priceline and Hotwire.com match flexible travelers with empty hotel rooms at budget prices.

Other London Websites: For more ideas, check out www.londontown. com, www.athomeinlondon.co.uk, wwww.londonbb.com, www. lastminute.com, www.visitlondon.com, and www.eurocheapo.com.

stay at least three nights, or simply ask if there are any cheaper rooms. Some of my recommended hotels offer a discount for those who use this book—it's worth asking when you reserve your room. Off-season (Nov-March), fearless negotiators can arrive without a reservation late on a slow day and start talking.

Besides hotels, there are cheaper alternatives. Bed-and-breakfasts (B&Bs) offer a personal touch at a fair price—www.londonbb.com is a good resource. Airbnb.com makes it reasonably easy to find a place to sleep in someone's home. All-ages hostels offer dorm beds (and a few inexpensive doubles) for £20-30 (sheets included) and come with curfews and other rules; try www.hostelworld.com.

Renting an apartment (a "flat") can save money if you're traveling as a family, staying more than a week, and planning to cook your own meals. Try www.vrbo.com, www.homeaway.com, www.perfectplaces.com, www. homefromhome.co.uk, www.london-house.com, or www.gowithit.co.uk.

Don't be too cheap when picking a hotel. In summer, pay a little more for air-conditioning. And remember that cheaper places in nondescript neighborhoods can be depressing. Your London experience will be more memorable with a welcoming oasis to call home.

VICTORIA STATION NEIGHBORHOOD: Central, safe, tidy, and full of decent eateries; close to Victoria Tube, bus, and train stations

$$$$ Lime Tree Hotel 135 Ebury Street tel. 020/7730-8191, www.limetreehotel.co.uk	Enthusiastically run, with spacious, stylish rooms and fun-loving breakfast room
$$$ B&B Belgravia 64 Ebury Street tel. 020/7259-8570, www.bb-belgravia.com	Bright but worn rooms with closets and above-average space, good value for the location
$$$ Luna Simone Hotel 47 Belgrave Road tel. 020/7834-5897, www.lunasimonehotel.com	Spacious, modern, and family-run, RS%, bus #24
$$ New England Hotel 20 Saint George's Drive tel. 020/7834-8351 www.newenglandhotel.com	Family-run, slightly worn but well-priced rooms in tight old corner building
$$ Best Western Victoria Palace 17 Belgrave Road tel. 020/7821-7113 www.bestwesternvictoriapalace.co.uk	Modern business-class comfort in two separate buildings, elevator
$$ Jubilee Hotel 31 Eccleston Square tel. 020/7834-0845, www.jubileehotel.co.uk	Well-run, colorful slumbermill, tiny rooms and beds, good value with RS%
$$ Bakers Hotel 126 Warwick Way tel. 020/7834-0729, www.bakershotel.co.uk	Well-worn, modest prices, tight rooms, good location, small breakfast, RS%
$ Cherry Court Hotel 23 Hugh Street tel. 020/7828-2840 www.cherrycourthotel.co.uk	Family-run, 12 tiny but bright rooms, air-con, breakfast in room, RS%
$ EasyHotel Victoria 34 Belgrave Road tel. 020/7834-1379, www.easyhotel.com	Modern-but-spartan chain hotel, super-cheap base price but you'll pay for all extras

SOUTH KENSINGTON: Quiet, classy, and upscale; conveniently located on Tube Circle Line

$$$$ Aster House 3 Sumner Place tel. 020/7581-5888, www.asterhouse.com	Friendly owners, sunny spaces, free loaner mobile phones, RS%

$$$$ Number Sixteen 16 Summer Place tel. 020/7589-5232, US tel. 888-559-5508 www.firmdalehotels.com	Over-the-top class, modern decor, plush lounges, honeymoon-perfect, soft prices, elevator
$$$$ The Pelham Hotel 15 Cromwell Place tel. 020/7589-8288, US tel. 888-757-5587 www.pelhamhotel.co.uk	Business-class hotel mixes pretense style and perks (gym); web specials, elevator

NOTTING HILL: Residential; trendy and popular with the young international set; Tube stops: Bayswater, Notting Hill, and Holland Park

$$$ Vancouver Studios 30 Prince's Square tel. 020/7243-1270 www.vancouverstudios.co.uk	Modern rooms with equipped kitchenettes rather than breakfast, nice garden, great value for this neighborhood
$$$ Phoenix Hotel 1 Kensington Gardens Square tel. 020/7229-2494, www.phoenixhotel.co.uk	Spacious public spaces, modern-feeling rooms, prices from fine value to rip-off, elevator
$$$ Princes Square Guest Accommodation 23 Prince's Square tel. 020/7229-9876 www.princessquarehotel.co.uk	Big, well-located, practical place, elevator, good value
$$$ Portobello Hotel 22 Stanley Gardens tel. 020/7727-2777, www.portobellohotel.com	Funky yet elegant rooms on a quiet, residential street
$$ Kensington Gardens Hotel 9 Kensington Gardens Square tel. 020/7243-7600 www.kensingtongardenshotel.co.uk	Pleasant rooms, many stairs and no elevator, breakfast next door, RS%
¢ Norwegian YWCA (Norsk K.F.U.K.) 52 Holland Park tel. 020/7727-9346, www.kfukhjemmet.org.uk	Some doubles, restrictions on age/nationality/gender, bargains worth a sex change

PADDINGTON STATION NEIGHBORHOOD: Not as charming, but offers all the travelers' amenities and convenient transportation connections

$$$ Tudor Court Hotel 10 Norfolk Square tel. 020/7723-5157 www.tudorcourtpaddington.co.uk	Colorful, tight rooms with plastic bathrooms and creaky plumbing, run by the Gupta family

Eating

England's reputation for miserable food—once well-deserved—is now history. The London cuisine scene is lively, trendy, and almost unbelievably diverse. Even traditional pub grub has gone "upmarket," offering fresh vegetables and pasta in place of greasy fries and mushy peas.

I've listed places by neighborhood—handy to your sightseeing and recommended hotels. (✪ See the restaurant maps on pages 182-185.) Because London can be expensive, I list a wide variety of eateries, from candlelit splurges to take-away fish-and-chips, with an emphasis on fun, moderately priced options.

Whether it's dining well with the upper-crust, sharing hearty pub fare with the blokes, or joining young secretaries at the sushi bar—eating out has become an essential part of the London experience.

Eating on London's Schedule

Traditionally, Brits have started their day with a large bacon-and-eggs breakfast. Nowadays most Londoners eat lighter, but most hotels still serve the traditional "fry-up," which tides many tourists over until dinner.

Lunch (12:00-14:00) is usually quick and simple—gobbling a pre-made sandwich while perched on a deli stool. Around 16:00, some Londoners still pause for the traditional tea and pastry break. After work, office drones pack London's pubs for an hour of power-drinking and noshing before the commute home. In the early evening, ethnic eateries buzz with the pre-theater crowd. After 19:00, the sit-down restaurants fill up with diners enjoying a romantic meal. Late at night, Londoners relax in the pubs for a pint, a chat, and a game of darts.

Restaurants

Traditional English fare is still served in classy, wood-paneled restaurants, but you'll find many more establishments featuring foods from around the world. All of Britain's eateries, including pubs that serve food, are now smoke-free. Get the latest on the ever-changing eating scene from weekly entertainment magazines (sold at newsstands), london-eating.co.uk, or squaremeal.co.uk.

London restaurants can be expensive when ordering a la carte. But portions are generally huge, and sharing is common. Couples could split a single main dish, a salad, and two drinks to make a filling meal.

Take advantage of fixed-price meals and specials for lunch and early-bird dinners. These can save as much as 50 percent on an a la carte meal in an elegant restaurant. (I've pointed out some deals in my listings.) Free tap water is always available.

Pub Grub

Your best bet for good, reasonably priced food is always the corner pub. Many of London's 7,000 pubs serve hearty lunches (roughly 12:00-14:00) and dinners (18:00-20:00) in friendly surroundings under ancient timbers for around £8-12. Standard items are fish-and-chips, "bangers and mash" (sausages and mashed potatoes), and meat pies. But many pubs now also have salad bars, quiche, hamburgers, "jacket potatoes" (baked potato with toppings), pasta, and curried dishes.

You generally order food at the bar—just ask the bartender, who can explain their pub's system. Don't tip unless the place has full table service.

Not all pubs serve meals, so look for pubs that proudly advertise their daily specials. For more pub grub listings, including upscale gastropubs (£12-18 meals), try www.thegoodpubguide.co.uk.

Pubs generally are open Monday through Saturday 11:00-23:00 and Sunday 12:00-22:30. Many stay open later, particularly on Friday and Saturday. For drinks, order your beer or other beverage at the bar and pay as you go, with no need to tip.

The pub is the heart of the people's England. Whether you're a teetotaler or a total beer-guzzler, they should be a part of your travel here. "Pub" is short for "public house." It's an extended living room. Get vocal with a local. Eat, drink, get out of the rain, and watch a soccer match. A cup of darts is free for the asking. Make a few friends and memories, and feel the pulse of London. Cheers!

Other Budget Alternatives

Ethnic Restaurants: Foods from around the world—often from Britain's former colonies—add spice to the London cuisine scene. Chinese, Thai, and Middle Eastern kebabs make healthy inexpensive meals; they're even cheaper if you order takeout. Eating Indian food is practically "going local" in cosmopolitan London. If you're not familiar with Indian food, consider an easy-to-order fixed-price combination. Couples could order two main dishes, plus rice, *naan* (flatbread), and an Indian beer for about £20.

Chain Restaurants: I know—you're going to Britain to enjoy little hole-in-the-wall pubs, so mass-produced food is the furthest thing from your mind. But several excellent chains can be a nice break from pub grub. My favorites are Pret (a.k.a. Pret à Manger), Wasabi, and Eat.

Pubs offer food, drink, and conversation.

Eating ethnic food is "going local" here.

Restaurant Price Code

$$$$ Splurge: Most main courses over £20
$$$ Pricier: £15-20
$$ Moderate: £10-15
$ Budget: Under £10

Based on the average cost of a typical main course. Drinks, desserts, and splurge items (steak and seafood) can raise the price considerably. Carryout fish-and-chips and other takeout food is **$**; a basic pub or sit-down eatery is **$$**; a gastropub or casual but more upscale restaurant is **$$$**; and a swanky splurge is **$$$$**.

Office workers crowd Pret and Eat for sandwiches, salads, and pastries. Wasabi is a bright Japanese chain that lets you assemble your own plate in a fun and efficient way. Byron Hamburgers is worth seeking out if you need a burger fix, as is Jamie's Italian for hip, upmarket pizza and pasta. Find excellent seafood at the Scottish chain Loch Fyne. Also popular are Itso (Japanese), Wagamama Noodle Bar (pan-Asian), Le Pain Quotidien (Belgian), Côte Brasserie (French), Masala Zone (Indian), and Busaba Eathai (Thai).

Museums: Handy on-site eateries are perfect for relaxing, and digesting all the art and culture you've taken in.

Picnics: Save time and money while enjoying London's fine park benches and polite pigeons. You can easily get prepared food to go: ethnic takeout, premade sandwiches, fish-and-chips, and hot-pocket-type meat pies called Cornish pasties (PASS-teez). Corner grocery chains (Sainsbury, Marks & Spencer, or Tesco) sell fruit, yogurt, trail mix, drinks, and picnic supplies. Pick up a world-class dessert at a bakery and enjoy your feast on an open-top bus tour or scenic cruise on the River Thames.

Some English Specialties

England's oft-maligned "cuisine" focuses on meat, potatoes, and dairy. At breakfast, sample interesting side dishes served with the bacon-and-eggs "fry-up"—grilled tomato, sautéed mushrooms, or baked beans. For lunch, try various meat pies such as steak-and-kidney or shepherd's (lamb) pie.

Taking Tea in London

Though fewer Brits these days make a big deal out of the midafternoon tea-and-biscuit break, many fancy restaurants and hotels offer this genteel tradition. You'll get a pot of tea with scones, jam, clotted (buttery) cream, and finger sandwiches, served in elegant, pinkiefinger surroundings.

Prices range from about £11 for a small-assortment "cream" tea to a bigger £20 "afternoon" tea, to £30 or more for a "high" tea that's almost a small dinner. Some places serve tea all afternoon (12:00-18:30), some only from around 15:00 to 17:30. Most welcome tourists in jeans and sneakers. Some of my favorite places include:

- **$$$ The Wolseley,** served in a classic former car showroom (160 Piccadilly Street, Tube: Piccadilly, £11.50-37.50, reserve at tel. 020/7499-6996 or www.thewolseley.com).
- **$$$$ The Orangery at Kensington Palace,** in its bright white hall near Princess Di's former residence. Take tea in the former princess' orangery or on the terrace (in orange brick building about 100 yards from Kensington Palace, £27.50-37.50, no reservations, tel. 020/3166-6113, www.hrp.org.uk).
- **$$$$ Fortnum & Mason** has several options: You can "Take Tea in the Parlour" for £23.50, enjoy the "Gallery Tea" for £26—or go all out in the Diamond Jubilee Tea Salon, royally priced at £40-44 (181 Piccadilly, reserve online or by phone at least a week ahead, tel. 020/7734-8040, www.fortnumandmason.com, dress up a bit).
- **$$$$ The Capital Hotel,** a luxury hotel near Harrods' with five intimate tables (22 Basil Street, Tube: Knightsbridge, £30, definitely reserve on weekends, tel. 020/7591-1202, www.capitalhotel.co.uk).
- **$$$ The National Dining Rooms and National Café,** two classy cafés in the National Gallery (located on Trafalgar Square, Tube: Charing Cross, walk-ins welcome, £15-17, tel. 020/7747-2525, www.peytonandbyrne.co.uk).

Eating

Desserts—care for some spotted dick? All hail English ale. Cheers!

For a full-blown dinner, enjoy roast beef with Yorkshire pudding (which is a pastry, not a pudding).

Desserts, or "sweets," include a variety of sponge cakes and "puddings" (breads) slathered in cream, custard, jam, or liqueur. Many come with colorful names like fool, trifle, castle pudding, or spotted dick. Scones are popular.

Beer is a national institution. Always order on tap, not bottled, preferably from the long-handled taps, indicating it comes from casks, not kegs. The British specialty is their amber-colored ales, served warmer and less carbonated than American- and German-style lagers. Most pubs offer a variety of ales, lagers, stouts (dark, like the Irish-made Guinness), ciders (strong taste and kick), and bitters (hop-flavored ales, perhaps the most typical British beer).

Wine bars—upscale pubs serving wines by the glass—have become essentially British, but virtually no wines are homegrown. For other spirits, gentlemen enjoy the "G and T" (gin and tonic), and ladies like the fruity cocktail-in-a-bottle called Pimm's or a refreshing half-beer/half-7-Up "shandy." No self-respecting bloke would order a Pimm's or a shandy. I order mine with quiche.

	St. Martin-in-the-Fields Café in the Crypt NE corner of Trafalgar Square, in church basement tel. 020/7766-1158	Tasty cafeteria line freshly stocked for breakfast, lunch, and dinner (Mon-Tue 8:00-20:00, Wed 8:00-22:30, Thu-Sat 8:00-21:00, Sun 11:00-18:00)
➋	**$$ The Chandos Pub's Opera Room** 29 St. Martin's Lane tel. 020/7836-1401	Fish-and-chips with locals in upstairs room overlooking Trafalgar tourist crush (daily 11:30-21:00, Fri until 18:00)
➌	**$$ Gordon's Wine Bar** Bottom of Villiers Street at #47 tel. 020/7930-1408	Candlelit 15th-century cellar packed with work crowd, small-dish buffet, great with port (Mon-Sat 11:00-23:00, Sun 12:00-22:00)
➍	**Harp Pub** 47 Chandos Place tel. 020/7836-0291	Local après-work favorite, no meals, drinks only (Mon-Sat 10:30-23:30, Sun 12:00-22:30)

CENTRAL LONDON—NEAR PICCADILLY (see map, page 182)

➎	**$$$ The Savini at the Criterion** 224 Piccadilly tel. 020/7930-0488 www.saviniatcriterion.co.uk	Palatial chandelier ambience in eye-pleasing old church; reasonable for lunch, drinks, before 19:00; smart to reserve (daily 12:00-14:30 & 17:30-23:30)
➏	**$$$$ The Wolseley** 160 Piccadilly tel. 020/7499-6996 www.thewolseley.com	Old-time formal elegance, unexceptional but reasonable Austrian/French cuisine and tea, reservations wise (daily 7:00-24:00)

CENTRAL LONDON—NEAR COVENT GARDEN (see map, page 182)

➐	**$$$$ Joe Allen** 13 Exeter Street tel. 020/7836-0651	Bustling candlelit basement, modern international and American cuisine, stylish theater crowd (daily 12:00-24:00, piano music after 19:00)
➑	**$$$ Loch Fyne** 2 Catherine Street tel. 020/7240-4999	Scottish franchise, homegrown shellfish, inviting no-pretense atmosphere, set-menu specials (long hours daily)

⑨	**$$$$ Rules Restaurant** 34 Maiden Lane tel. 020/7836-5314 www.rules.co.uk	Classy, plush Edwardian atmosphere with formal service and gamey menu (daily 12:00-23:00)
⑩	**$$$ Sitar Indian Restaurant** Next to Somerset House at 149 Strand tel. 020/7836-3730	Small and dressy, with efficient service, fine fish, £15 vegetarian thali (Mon-Fri 12:00-14:30 & 17:30-23:30, Sat 15:00-23:30)
⑪	**$$$ Union Jacks** Inside Covent Garden market hall tel. 020/3640-7086	Jamie Oliver venture, traditional British ingredients fused into inventive modern dishes (daily 12:00-23:00)
⑫	**$$ Lamb and Flag Pub** 33 Rose Street tel. 020/7497-9504	Spit-and-sawdust pub serving traditional grub since 1772 and a favorite of Charles Dickens (long hours daily)
⑬	**$$$ Dishoom** 7 Boundary Street tel. 020/7420-9324	Hotspot for upmarket Indian cuisine, line up early for best seating (Mon-Fri 8:00-23:00, Sat-Sun 8:00-21:00)
⑭	**$$$ Belgo Centraal** One block north of Covent Garden Tube station at 50 Earlham Street tel. 020/7813-2233	Belgian mussels and chips in vast, underground beer-hall (daily 12:00-23:00)

CENTRAL LONDON—NEAR SOHO AND CHINATOWN (see map, page 182)

⑮	**$$ Wong Kei** 41 Wardour Street tel. 020/7437-8408	Locals endure waiter abuse for satisfying BBQ rice dishes or hot pots, cash only (daily 11:30-23:30)
⑯	**Gelupo Gelato** **7 Archer Street** tel. 020/7287-5555	Creative and delicious homemade dessert favorites (daily 11:00-23:00, Sun from 12:00)
⑰	**$$ Princi** 135 Wardour Street tel. 020/7478-8888	Popular Italian deli, communal table or to-go (Mon-Sat 8:00-24:00, Sun from 10:00)
⑱	**$$$ Bocca di Lupo** 12 Archer Street tel. 020/7734-2223 www.boccadilupo.com	Pricey dressy Italian, fun counter seating, build a meal with small plates, reservations wise (Mon-Sat 12:00-15:00 & 17:30-23:00, Sun until 21:00)

⑲	**$$ Y Ming Chinese Restaurant** 35 Greek Street tel. 020/7734-2721	Dressy European decor, authentic northern Chinese fare (Mon-Sat 12:00-23:45, closed Sun)
⑳	**$$ Ducksoup** 41 Dean Street tel. 020/7287-4599	Upscale but relaxed wine bar, select modern British dishes (Mon-Sat 12:00-22:30, Sun until 17:00)
㉑	**$$$ Andrew Edmunds Restaurant** 46 Lexington Street tel. 020/7437-5708	Tiny candlelit local find, modern European cuisine, reserve ground floor table (Mon-Sat 12:30-15:30 & 17:30-22:45, Sun 13:00-16:00 & 18:00-22:30)
㉒	**$$ Mildred's Vegetarian Restaurant** 45 Lexington Street tel. 020/7494-1634	Enjoyable menu, pleasant interior, vegan options, happy eaters (Mon-Sat 12:00-23:00, closed Sun)
㉓	**$$ Bi Bim Bap** 11 Greek Street tel. 020/7287-3434	Popular and muggy little diner named for what it sells: bibimbap ("mixed rice") (Mon-Fri 12:00-15:00 & 18:00-23:00, Sat 12:00-23:00, closed Sun)
㉔	**$$$ The Gay Hussar** 2 Greek Street tel. 020/7437-0973	What may be England's only Hungarian restaurant, dressy and tight, traditional Hungarian fare (Mon-Sat 12:15-14:30 & 17:30-22:45, closed Sun)

THE CITY, AROUND ST. PAUL'S (see map, page 184)

㉕	**$ The Counting House** 50 Cornhill, east of St. Paul's, near Mansion House tel. 020/7283-7123	Sandwiches, meat pies, fish, fresh vegetables (Mon-Fri 9:00-23:00, closed Sat-Sun)
㉖	**$ Ye Olde Cheshire Cheese** 145 Fleet Street tel. 020/7353-6170	1667 tavern once served pub grub to Dickens, Samuel Johnson, Yeats (open daily)
㉗	**$ The Black Friar** 174 Queen Victoria Street tel. 020/7236-5474	Great Art Nouveau decor (c. 1900-1915) and traditional pub fare (Mon-Sat 9:00-23:00, Sun 12:00-22:30, food daily until 22:00)
㉘	**$$$ The Old Bank of England** 194 Fleet Street tel. 020/7430-2255	Pub in lavish old bank building (Mon-Fri 11:00-23:00, food until 21:00, closed Sat-Sun)

NOTTING HILL (see map, page 184)	
㉙ **$$$$ Maggie Jones's** 6 Old Court Place tel. 020/7937-6462 www.maggie-jones.co.uk	Solid English cuisine, rustic but jazzy ambience, splittable meat pies (daily 12:00-14:30 & 18:00-23:00, reservations recommended)
㉚ **$ The Churchill Arms and Thai Kitchen** 119 Kensington Church St. tel. 020/7792-1246	Old-English pub grub in front, hearty Thai in back, packed evenings (daily 12:00-22:00)
㉛ **$ The Prince Edward** 73 Prince's Square, 2 blocks north of Bayswater Road tel. 020/7727-2221	Cut-above grub in classic pub setting, indoor or sidewalk tables (daily 10:30-23:00)
㉜ **$ Café Diana** 5 Wellington Terrace tel. 020/7792-9606	Healthy Middle Eastern pita sandwiches, salads, and meals (daily 8:00-23:00, cash only)
㉝ **$$ Royal China Restaurant** 13 Queensway tel. 020/7221-2535	Pricey favorite for dress-up Chinese locals, dim sum until 17:00 (Mon-Sat 12:00-23:00, Sun 11:00-22:00)
㉞ **$ Whiteleys Shopping Centre Food Court** Corner of Queensway and Porchester Gardens	Options include Yo! Sushi, Café Rouge, pizza, Starbucks (daily 8:30-24:00)
㉟ **Tesco Supermarket** 114 Notting Hill Gate	Grocery store (Mon-Sat 7:00-23:00, Sun 12:00-18:00)
SOUTH KENSINGTON (see map, page 185)	
㊱ **$$ Exhibition Road Eateries** On the Victoria and Albert Museum side of the South Kensington Tube station	Block-long, traffic-free pedestrian zone lined with enticing little eateries, including Fernandez and Wells, Thai Square, Casa Brindisa, and others
㊲ **$$$ Moti Mahal Indian Restaurant** 3 Glendower Place tel. 020/7584-8428	Bangladeshi, mod ambience, good service, try spicy chicken *jalfrezi* (daily 12:00-14:30 & 17:30-23:30)
㊳ **$$ Beirut Express** 65 Old Brompton Road tel. 020/7591-0123	Fresh Lebanese cuisine, cheap take-away in front, restaurant in back (daily 12:00-23:00)

Eating

❸❾	**$ Bosphorus Kebabs** 59 Old Brompton Road tel. 020/7584-4048	Student favorite for quick hearty Turkish meals and kebabs (daily 10:30-24:00)
❹⓿	**$$ Rocca di Papa** 73 Old Brompton Road tel. 020/7225-3413	Bright and dressy Italian place with heated terrace; £8 pizza, pasta, or salad (daily 11:30-23:30)
❹❶	**$$$ The Anglesea Arms** 15 Selwood Terrace tel. 020/7373-7960	Destination gourmet pub, great terrace, mellow woody ambience (meals served daily 12:00-15:00 & 18:00-22:00)
❹❷	**Tesco Express** 50 Old Brompton Road	Grocery store open long hours daily
❹❸	**$ Franco Manca** 91 Old Brompton Road tel. 020/7584-9713	Taverna-inspired pizzeria, organic ingredients, typical Italian charm (daily 11:30-23:00)

VICTORIA STATION NEIGHBORHOOD (see map, page 185)

❹❹	**$$$ Ebury Wine Bar** 139 Ebury Street tel. 020/7730-5447 www.eburyrestaurant.co.uk	Cut-above pub grub at bar, plus delightful $$$$ back room for modern European cuisine with a French accent (daily 12:00-14:45 & 18:00-22:15)
❹❺	**$ La Bottega** Corner of Ebury and Eccleston Streets tel. 020/7730-2730	Upscale Italian deli for fresh pastas, salads, sandwiches, to go or stay (Mon-Fri 8:00-17:30, Sat-Sun 9:00-18:00)
❹❻	**$$ The Duke of Wellington** 63 Eaton Terrace tel. 020/7730-1782	Classic neighborhood pub, forgettable grub, woodsy sidewalk seating, inviting interior (food served Mon-Sat 12:00-15:00 & 18:00-21:00, Sun lunch only)
❹❼	**$$$ The Thomas Cubitt** 44 Elizabeth Street tel. 020/7730-6060 www.thethomascubitt.co.uk	Trendy gastropub for young professionals, small-plate bar menu or pricey meals; smart to reserve (daily 12:00-22:00)
❹❽	**$$$ Grumbles** 35 Churton Street tel. 020/7834-0149 www.grumblesrestaurant.co.uk	Unpretentious cozy booths, excellent traditional English dishes, early bird specials; smart to reserve (daily 12:00-14:30 & 18:00-23:00)

㊾	**$$ Pimlico Fresh** 86 Wilton Road tel. 020/7932-0030	Breakfast and lunch, organic ingredients, good coffee, fresh-squeezed juices (Mon-Fri 7:30-19:30—breakfast until 15:00; Sat-Sun 9:00-18:00)
㊿	**$$ Seafresh Fish Restaurant** 80 Wilton Road tel. 020/7828-0747	Family-run, classic and creative fish-and-chips (Mon-Fri 12:00-15:00 & 17:00-22:30, Sat 12:00-22:30, closed Sun)
(51)	**$$ The Jugged Hare** 172 Vauxhall Bridge Road tel. 020/7828-1543	Vivid pub scene in old bank building, traditional grub plus modern veggies (food served daily 12:00-21:00)
(52)	**$$ St. George's Tavern** Corner of Hugh Street and Belgrave Road tel. 020/7630-1116	First-rate pub, eat inside or out, try "toad in the hole" sausages (Mon-Sat 10:00-22:00, Sun until 21:30)
(53) (54)	**M & S Simply Food** and **Sainsbury's Local** Located inside Victoria Station	Two grocery stores with long hours daily

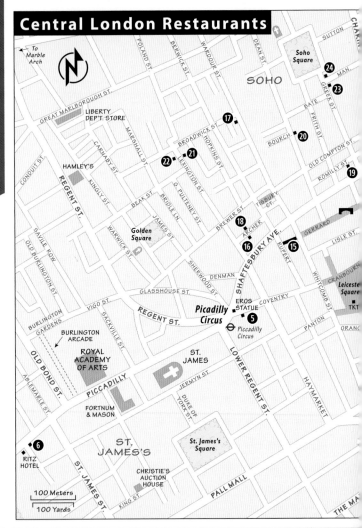

Central London Restaurants

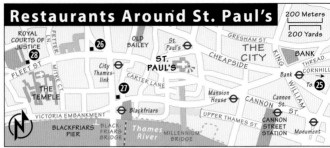

Restaurants Around St. Paul's

200 Meters
200 Yards

ROYAL COURTS OF JUSTICE
28
FETTER LA.
FLEET ST.
MITRE CT.
City Thameslink
OLD BAILEY
26
CARTER LANE
27
St. Paul's
ST. PAUL'S
GRESHAM ST
CHEAPSIDE
THE CITY
KING ST
BANK
THREAD.
Bank
CORNHILL
To **25**
WILLIAM ST
Mansion House
CANNON ST.
Cannon St.
VICTORIA EMBANKMENT
Blackfriars
UPPER THAMES ST.
CANNON STREET STATION
BLACKFRIARS PIER
BLACKFRIARS BRIDGE
Thames River
MILLENNIUM BRIDGE
THE TEMPLE
Monument

Notting Hill Restaurants

200 Meters
200 Yards

WESTBOURNE GROVE
PEMBRIDGE VILLAS
CHEPSTOW PL.
HEREFORD RD.
Leinster Square
Prince's Square
31
Kensington Gardens Square
34
POST
PORCHESTER GARDENS
QUEENSBOROUGH TERR.
BAYSWATER
DAWSON PL.
ST PETERSBURGH PL.
Bayswater
Moscow RD.
QUEENSWAY
SATURDAY MARKET
Pembridge Square
PORTOBELLO RD.
PEMBRIDGE RD.
OSSINGTON ST.
PALACE CT.
BARK PL.
33
To Marble Arch
KENSINGTON PARK RD.
NOTTING HILL
32
Queensway
BAYSWATER RD.
UXBRIDGE
Notting Hill Gate
NOTTING HILL GATE
KENSINGTON PL.
35
KENSINGTON CHURCH ST.
PLAYGROUND
BROAD WALK
Kensington Gardens
CAMPDEN HILL RD.
PEEL ST.
CAMPDEN ST.
30
BEDFORD GARDENS
SHEFFIELD TERR.
HORTON ST.
KENSINGTON
HOLLAND ST.
BRUNSWICK GDNS.
KENSINGTON PALACE GARDENS
PALACE GARDENS TERR.
Round Pond
KENSINGTON PALACE
OLD CT. PL.
29
PALACE AVE.
PALACE GREEN
KENSINGTON RD.

South Kensington Restaurants

NATURAL HISTORY MUSEUM

VICTORIA & ALBERT MUSEUM

BROMPTON

CROMWELL RD.

EXHIBITION RD.

QUEEN'S

QUEENS-BURY PL.

CROMWELL PL.

THURLOE PL.

Thurloe Square

BROMPTON RD.

WALTON ST.

HASKER ST.

MILNER ST.

HARR. RD.

REECE MEWS

South Kens.

36

THUR. ST.

PELHAM ST.

PELHAM CRES.

LUGAN PL.

PRAYCOTT AVE.

SLOANE AVE.

QUEEN'S GATE

37

42

POST

OLD BROMPTON RD.

43 **40** **38** **39**

Onslow Square

ONSLOW SQ.

SUMNER PL.

SOUTH KENSINGTON

ONSLOW GARDENS

FULHAM RD.

SYDNEY ST.

41

300 Meters

300 Yards

Victoria Station Neighborhood Restaurants

EATON PL.

Eaton Square

BELGRAVE PL.

ECCLESTON ST.

BELGRAVE ST.

GROSVENOR GARDENS

LWR.

VICTORIA ST.

LITTLE BEN

53

Victoria

CARLISLE PL.

VAUXHALL BRIDGE RD.

THIRLEBY RD.

WESTMINSTER CATHEDRAL

BELGRAVIA

EATON SQ.

CHESTER ROW

Chester Square

45

EBURY ST.

ECCLESTON PL.

PALACE RD.

VICTORIA STATION

WILTON RD.

FRANCIS ST.

WILLOW PL.

VINCENT SQUARE

46

S. EATON PL.

47

44

ELIZABETH ST.

POST

ECCLESTON BRIDGE

ECCLESTON ST.

GILLINGHAM ST.

GUILDHOUSE ST.

WILTON RD.

LONGMORE

GILLINGHAM ST.

51

EATON TERR.

SEMLEY PL.

P

COACH (BUS) STN.

SHOPS

52

HIGH ST.

BELGRAVE RD.

DENBIGH ST.

50

49

TACHBROOK ST.

BOURNE ST.

EBURY ST.

CUNDY ST.

BUCKINGHAM

Ebury Square

Eccleston Square

ST. GEORGE'S DR.

WARWICK WAY

CLARENDON ST.

48

PIMLICO RD.

200 Meters

200 Yards

PIMLICO RD.

ALDERNEY ST.

ST.

CAMBRIDGE ST.

Warwick Square

GLOUCESTER ST.

CHURTON ST.

CHARLWOOD ST.

To Pimlico & Tate Britain

Practicalities

Rick Steves | Pocket London

PLANNING

London's best travel months are July and August, with the best weather, daylight from 6:30-22:00, and the full range of tourist activities. "Shoulder season" (May-June, Sept-early Oct) has slightly smaller crowds and slightly better hotel prices, and the weather is decent. London makes a great winter getaway, especially during Christmas season. Although it's dark and drizzly, you'll find fewer crowds. The pubs are cozy, and the city feels lively but not touristy. No matter when you go, plan for rain.

Make sure your passport is up-to-date (to renew, see www.travel.state.gov). Call your debit- and credit-card companies about your plans. Book hotel rooms well in advance, especially for peak season (July-Aug) and holidays. Consider buying travel insurance. If you're traveling beyond London, research railpasses, Eurostar train reservations, and car rentals.

MONEY

One British pound (£1) = about $1.40. To convert pounds to dollars add 40 percent: £20 = about $28, £50 = about $70. (Check www.oanda.com for the latest exchange rates.) The pound, also called a "quid," is broken into 100 pence (p).

Withdraw money from an ATM (often called a "cashpoint" in Britain) using a debit card, just like at home. Visa and MasterCard are commonly used throughout Europe. Before departing, call your bank or credit-card company: Ask about international transaction fees, alert them that you'll be making withdrawals in Europe, and get your credit card's PIN. Many travelers bring a second debit/credit card as a backup.

While American credit cards are accepted almost everywhere in Europe, even newer chip-style cards may not work in some payment machines (e.g., ticket kiosks). Be prepared to pay with cash, find a nearby cashier, or try entering your credit card's PIN.

To keep your valuables safe, wear a money belt. But if you do lose your credit or debit card, report the loss immediately with a phone call: Visa (tel. 303/967-1096), MasterCard (tel. 636/722-7111), and American Express (tel. 336/393-1111).

Helpful Websites

London Tourist Information: www.visitlondon.com
Britain Tourist Information: www.visitbritain.com
Passports and Red Tape: www.travel.state.gov
Cheap Flights: www.kayak.com (for international flights), www.skyscanner.net (for flights within Europe)
Airplane Carry-on Restrictions: www.tsa.gov or www.dft.gov.uk
London Entertainment and Current Events: www.timeout.com/london or www.londontown.com
European Train Schedules: www.bahn.com
General Travel Tips: www.ricksteves.com (helpful info on trip planning, train travel, rail passes, car rental, travel insurance, packing lists, and much more—plus updates to this book)

ARRIVAL IN LONDON

By Plane

One of the world's busiest airports, **Heathrow** has five terminals, T-1 through T-5. Each terminal has all the necessary travelers' services (info desks, ATMs, shops, eateries, etc.). You can travel between terminals on free trains and buses, but it can be time-consuming—plan ahead if you'll need to change terminals (LHR, tel. 0844-335-180, www.heathrow.com). To get between Heathrow and downtown London (14 miles away), you have several options:

Taxi: The one-hour trip costs £45-75 to west and central London, for up to four people.

Tube: For £5-6, the Tube takes you from any Heathrow terminal to downtown London in 50-60 minutes on the Piccadilly Line (6/hour). Follow signs in the terminal to the Tube station. If you plan to use the Tube for transport in London, buy a Travelcard or pay-as-you-go Oyster card covering Zone 1-2 (central London); you'll pay a small supplement for the Heathrow-to-London portion.

Train: From T-2 and T-3, the Heathrow Connect train goes to Paddington Station (£10.20 one-way, 2/hour, 40 minutes, toll tel. 0345-604-1515, www.heathrowconnect.com). From T-1, T-3, and T-5, the Heathrow

Express goes to Paddington (£22, 4/hour, 15-20 minutes, toll tel. 0845-600-1515, www.heathrowexpress.co.uk). Transfers from T-4 are free.

Bus: Buses depart from the outdoor common area called the Central Bus Station, a five-minute walk from T-2/T-3. National Express buses go to Victoria Coach Station near the Victoria train and Tube station (£6-9, 1-2/hour, 45-75 minutes, toll tel. 0871-781-8181, www.nationalexpress.com).

Shuttle: Shared minivans link Heathrow with London hotels (works best going from your hotel to the airport).

From London to Heathrow: Confirm in advance which terminal your flight will use, to avoid having to transfer between terminals. If it's T-4 or T-5, allow extra time. If arriving by Tube, note that not every Piccadilly Line train stops at every terminal: Make sure your train is going to the terminal you want. Hotels can often line up a cab back to the airport for about £50. Taxi drivers generally know which terminal you'll need based on the airline, but bus drivers may not.

Gatwick and London's Other Airports: Gatwick is London's second-biggest airport (LGW, toll tel. 0844-892-0322, www.gatwickairport.com). Gatwick Express trains shuttle conveniently to Victoria Station (£20, Oyster cards accepted, 4/hour, 30 minutes, toll tel. 0845-850-1530, www.gatwickexpress.com). To connect Gatwick and Heathrow, use the National Express bus (£25, 1.5 hours but allow at least three hours between flights, toll tel. 0871-781-8178, www.nationalexpress.com).

London's other, lesser airports are Stansted Airport (STN, toll tel. 0844-335-1803, www.stanstedairport.com), Luton Airport (LTN, tel. 01582/405-100, www.london-luton.co.uk), and London City Airport (LCY, tel. 020/7646-0088, www.londoncityairport.com).

Heathrow Airport—busy and efficient

From Heathrow to downtown on the Tube

By Train

There are nine main stations, each serving a different region. For example, to go to Paris on the Eurostar, you leave from St. Pancras International. Trains to Heathrow, Windsor, or Bath leave from Paddington. You can make reservations and buy tickets for any destination at any train station.

For schedules, tickets, and general information on British trains, call 0845-748-4950 or visit www.nationalrail.co.uk. The best all-Europe train schedule information is at www.bahn.de. To see if a rail pass could save you money, check www.ricksteves.com/rail.

Eurostar: High-speed trains from St. Pancras International zip you under the English Channel to Paris or Brussels in 2.5 hours and to Amsterdam in just under 4 hours. Prices can range from $450 (first-class full-fare tickets) to less than $100 (second-class, non-refundable specials), so do your research and book ahead for the best deals (see www.rick-steves.com/eurostar or www.eurostar.com).

By Bus—Victoria Coach Station: For travel beyond London, buses are a cheaper—but considerably slower—option than the train. Most depart from Victoria Coach Station, a long block south of Victoria Station (Tube: Victoria, toll tel. 0871-781-8178 or www.nationalexpress.com).

By Cruise Ship

Cruise ships dock at Southampton (80 miles southwest of London) and Dover (80 miles southeast of London). Each is about a 1.5-hour drive or train ride to London. If you don't want to bother with public transportation, most cruise lines offer transit-only excursion packages into London. A taxi to central London costs around £125-150 one-way. The cheapest option from either port is to take a taxi to the town's train station, where trains run hourly to London.

HELPFUL HINTS

Tourist Information (TI): The City of London Information Centre is London's only publicly funded (and therefore impartial) "real" TI (Mon-Sat 9:30-17:30, Sun 10:00-16:00, just south of St. Paul's Cathedral, Tube: St. Paul's, tel. 020/7332-1456, www.visitthecity.co.uk). It sells Oyster cards, London Passes, skip-the-queue "Fast Track" sightseeing tickets (described on page 200), and some National Express bus tickets. It also stocks the helpful **London Planner,** a free monthly that lists all the sights, events, and hours. Other so-called tourist information offices around town are actually for-profit travel agencies, but they can be helpful. The best travel bookstores are Stanfords (12 Long Acre, Tube: Leicester Square, www. stanfords.co.uk) and Waterstone's (locations on both Piccadilly and Trafalgar Squares). The **Bensons London Street Map** is my favorite. Visit London, which serves the greater London area, doesn't have an office you can visit in person—but does have an information-packed website (www.visitlondon.com).

Time: Britain's time zone is one hour earlier than most of continental Europe, which makes it five/eight hours ahead of the east/west coasts of the US.

Business Hours: Most stores are open Monday through Saturday (roughly 10:00-17:00), with a late night on Wednesday or Thursday (until 19:00 or 20:00), depending on the neighborhood. On Sunday, when some stores are closed, street markets are lively with shoppers. Handy hole-in-the-wall grocery stores stay open late every day.

Holidays and Weekends: London's always-busy sights are inundated on three-day weekends, especially Bank Holidays on the first and last Mondays in May, and the last Monday in August. For a good list, see www.visitlondon.com/travel/public-holidays.

Watt's Up? Britain's electrical system operates on 220 volts (rather than 110 in the US) and uses plugs with three square prongs (rather than America's two slots or continental Europe's two round prongs). You'll need a three-prong adapter plug, sold inexpensively at travel stores in the US, and in British airports and drugstores. Most newer electronics automatically convert the voltage, so you won't need a separate converter.

Numbers and Stumblers: What Americans call the second floor of a building is the first floor in Europe. Europeans write dates as day/month/year. Britain uses a mix of "our" Imperial system (pounds, miles) and the metric system: A kilogram is 2.2 pounds; a liter is about a quart; and a kilometer is six-tenths of a mile. The British measure temperature in Celsius. 0°C = 32°F. For a rough conversion from Celsius to Fahrenheit, double the number and add 30.

Discounts: Many British sights, buses, and trains offer discounts (called "concessions" or "concs") for seniors (loosely defined as those who

Tipping

Tipping in Britain isn't as generous as it is in the US. In restaurants (or pubs with table service), if a service charge is included in the bill, it's not necessary to tip; if not, tip about 10-12.5 percent. At pubs where you order at the counter, you don't have to tip. To tip the cabbie, round up a bit (for a £4.50 fare, pay £5). In general, if someone in the tourism or service industry does a super job for you, a small tip of a pound or so is appropriate...but not required.

are retired or willing to call themselves a senior), children, families, and students and teachers with an international ID card (see www.isic.org).

Pedestrian Safety: Cars drive on the left side of the road—which can be as confusing for foreign pedestrians as for foreign drivers. Before crossing a street, I always look right, look left, then look right again just to be sure. Most crosswalks are even painted with instructions, reminding foreign guests to "Look right" or "Look left."

Useful Apps: City Maps 2Go ($2, available from iTunes) gives you good searchable maps even when you're not online. The MX Apps free Tube map (www.mxapps.co.uk) provides live updates on transit delays (when you're online), and shows the easiest way to connect station A to station B (even when you're not online). Time Out's free "Make Your City Amazing"" app has the latest on theater, museums, movies, and more (www.timeout.com/London).

Hurdling the Language Barrier: Don't get fagged or wound up over the twee, homely way Joe Bloggs can witter on. I mean, Bob's your uncle, we speak the same language. But if you do have trouble decoding how the English speak English, ✪ see the British-Yankee Vocabulary list on page 210. And please...don't call your waist pack a "fanny pack."

GETTING AROUND LONDON

In London, you're never more than a 10-minute walk from a stop on the metro/subway system (called the Tube). Buses are also convenient, and

...verywhere. For more information on routes, tickets, and passes, ...ov.uk.

...ng Tickets and Public-Transit Passes

...dividual paper tickets for the the Tube are ridiculously expensive (£4.90 per Tube ride). Save money with one of London's transit passes, which cover both the Tube and the bus system.

Oyster Card: This pay-as-you-go plastic card lets you travel at about half the price per ride as single Tube or bus tickets. You pay a £5 deposit when you buy the card, then load it up with credit. With the card, one ride in zones 1 and 2 during peak time is £2.90. When your balance gets low, you simply add credit—or "top up"—at a ticket window or machine. To use it, simply touch the card to the yellow card reader at the turnstile or entrance. It flashes green, and the fare is automatically deducted. Remember to tap your card again to "touch out" when you exit. An automatic price cap guarantees you'll never pay more than £6.50 in one day for rides within Zones 1 and 2.

One-Day Travelcard: This pass gives unlimited one-day travel on the Tube and buses in Zones 1-4 for £12.10. (The cheaper off-peak version is good for travel after 9:30 on weekdays and anytime on weekends.) To use it, feed the Travelcard into the Tube turnstile like a paper ticket (and retrieve it), or show it to the bus driver.

Seven-Day Travelcard: For £32.40 (plus a £5 deposit), you get a week's worth of travel in zones 1-2. It's comes as a paper version or can be added to an Oyster card.

Which Pass Is Best? On a short visit (three days or fewer), get an Oyster card with £20-25 of credit (£6.50 daily cap times three days, plus a

Go with the flow on London's mass transit.

Bus tours are worthwhile if traffic isn't bad.

An Oyster transit pass can save money.

Master London's transit, and go, go, go!

little extra for any rides outside Zones 1-2). If you're in London for five days or longer, the Seven-Day Travelcard will likely pay for itself.

Buy Oyster cards and Travelcards at any Tube station, from a ticket window or vending machine. All of these passes cover the Tube and bus system within Zones 1 and 2—an area that stretches beyond the Circle Line and includes virtually all recommended sights.

By Tube

Called the Tube or Underground (but never "subway"), one of this planet's great people-movers runs Monday through Saturday about 5:00-24:00, Sunday about 7:00-23:00.

Begin by studying the Tube map on the foldout map at the back of this book. Each line has a name (such as Circle, Northern, or Bakerloo) and two directions (indicated by the end-of-the-line stops). Find the line that will take you to your destination, and figure out roughly what direction (north, south, east, or west) you'll need to go to get there.

In the Tube station, use your Oyster card, Travelcard, or ticket to pass through the turnstile. Find your train by following signs to your line and the direction it's headed (such as *Central Line: East*). Since some tracks are shared by several lines, read signs on the platform to confirm that the approaching train is going to your specific destination. Transfers to another train are free, until you reach your final destination. You'll need your Oyster, Travelcard, or ticket to pass through the exit turnstile. Save walking time by choosing the best street exit—check the maps on the walls or ask any station personnel.

Rush hours (8:00-10:00 and 16:00-19:00) can be packed and sweaty. Be prepared to walk significant distances within Tube stations and ride long escalators (stand on the right to let others pass). Delays are common; bring

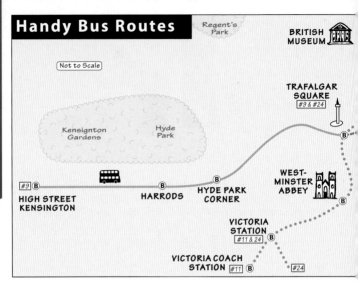

Handy Bus Routes

Regent's Park

BRITISH MUSEUM

Not to Scale

TRAFALGAR SQUARE
#9 & #24

Kensignton Gardens

Hyde Park

WEST-MINSTER ABBEY

#9

HIGH STREET KENSINGTON

HARRODS

HYDE PARK CORNER

VICTORIA STATION
#11 & 24

VICTORIA COACH STATION #11

#24

something to pass the time. A general rule of thumb is that it takes 30 minutes to travel six Tube stops (including walking time within stations). Be wary of thieves, especially amid the jostle of boarding and leaving crowded trains.

By Bus

London's excellent bus system works like buses anywhere. Every bus stop has a name, and every bus is headed to one end-of-the-line stop or the other. You can't buy single-trip tickets for buses, and you can't use cash to pay for your fare when boarding. Instead, you must have an Oyster card, a Travelcard, or a one-day Bus & Tram Pass (£5). If you're using your Oyster card, any bus ride in downtown London costs £1.50 (with a cap of £4.50 per day).

As you board, show your pass or Travelcard to the driver, or touch your Oyster card to the card reader. There's no need to tap your card or show your pass when you hop off. If you have an Oyster card or Travelcard, save your feet and use the bus, even just to get to a Tube stop. Check the bus stop closest to your hotel—it might be convenient to your sightseeing

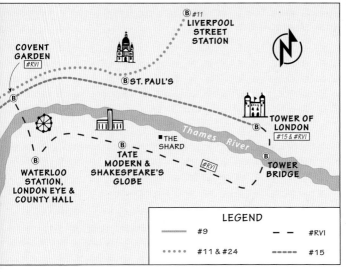

COVENT GARDEN
#RV1

#11
LIVERPOOL STREET STATION

N

B ST. PAUL'S

TOWER OF LONDON
#15 & #RV1

Thames River

THE SHARD

#RV1

TATE MODERN & SHAKESPEARE'S GLOBE

TOWER BRIDGE

WATERLOO STATION, LONDON EYE & COUNTY HALL

LEGEND

▬▬▬	#9	– –	#RV1
•••••	#11 & #24	▬ ▬ ▬	#15

plans. But during bump-and-grind rush hours (8:00-10:00 and 16:00-19:00), you'll go faster by Tube.

A few bus routes (see the map) are especially handy to sights and recommended hotels:

Route #9: High Street Kensington to Knightsbridge (Harrods) to Hyde Park Corner to Trafalgar Square to Aldwych (Somerset House).

Route #11: Victoria Station to Westminster Abbey to Trafalgar Square to St. Paul's and Liverpool Street Station and the East End.

Route #15: Trafalgar Square to St. Paul's to Tower of London (sometimes with heritage "Routemaster" old-style double-decker buses).

Route #24: Victoria Station to Westminster Abbey to Trafalgar Square to Euston Square, then north to Camden Town and Hampstead Heath.

Route #RV1: A scenic South Bank joyride from the Tower of London to the London Eye, then back across the Thames to Covent Garden.

By Taxi

London is the best taxi town in Europe. Big, black, carefully regulated cabs are everywhere. They know every nook and cranny in town. I've never met a crabby London cabbie.

If a cab's top light is on, just wave it down—even cabs going the opposite way—or find the nearest taxi stand. Telephoning a cab will get you one in minutes, but costs a little more (tel. 0871-871-8710).

Rides start at £2.40. The rate goes up about 20 percent after 20:00, and another 20 percent after 22:00. All extra charges are explained in writing on the cab wall. Tip a cabbie by rounding up (maximum 10 percent).

A typical daytime trip—from Trafalgar Square to St. Paul's—costs about £8-10. All cabs can carry five passengers, and some take six, for the same cost as a single traveler. So for a short ride, three adults in a cab travel at close to Tube prices. Avoid cabs when traffic is bad—they're slow and expensive, because the meter keeps running even at a standstill.

By Uber

Uber faces legal challenges in London and may not be operating when you visit. If Uber is running, it can be much cheaper than a taxi and is a handy alternative if there's a long line for a taxi or if no cabs are available. Uber drivers generally don't know the city as well as regular cabbies, and they don't have the access to some fast lanes that taxis do. Still, if you like using Uber, it can work great here.

STAYING CONNECTED

Bring your own mobile device (phone, tablet, laptop) and follow my budget tips. For more information than what I've provided here, see www.ricksteves.com/phoning.

Making Calls

To call Britain from the US or Canada: Dial 011-44 and then the local number, without the initial zero (011 is our international access code; 44 is Britain's country code).

To call Britain from a European country: Dial 00-44 followed by the local number, without the initial zero (00 is Europe's international access code).

To call within Britain: For local calls, just dial the local number (without the area code); for long-distance, dial the area code (including the initial 0) and the local number.

Useful Phone Numbers

Police and Ambulance: Tel. 999
Operator Assistance: Tel. 100 (free)
Directory Assistance: Toll tel. 118-811 (£0.50 flat rate from a landline; more from a mobile)
International Operator Assistance: Tel. 155 (free)
US Consulate and Embassy: Tel. 020/7499-9000, no walk-in passport services, Canada House, Trafalgar Square, Tube: Bond Street, London, http://london.usembassy.gov
Canadian High Commission: Tel. 020/7004-6000, passport services available Mon-Fri 9:30-12:30, 38 Grosvenor Street, Tube: Charing Cross, www.unitedkingdom.gc.ca
Toll-Free Numbers: Any number that begins with 0800 (but not others, such as 0845 or 0870) is toll-free.
Collect Calls to the US: Dial 0-800-89-0011. Press zero or stay on the line for an operator.

To call from Britain to another country: Dial 00, the country code (for example, 1 for the US or Canada), the area code, and the number. If you're calling European countries whose phone numbers begin with 0, you'll usually have to omit that 0 when you dial.

If you're calling from Britain (or elsewhere in Europe) using your US mobile phone, you may need to dial as if you're calling from the US.

Budget Tips for Using a Mobile Device in Europe

Use free Wi-Fi whenever possible. Unless you have an unlimited data plan, save most of your online tasks for Wi-Fi. Many hotels and cafés have Wi-Fi for guests.

Sign up for an international plan. Most providers offer a global plan that cuts the cost of calls and texts, and gives you a block of data. Your normal plan may already include this coverage (T-Mobile's does).

Minimize the use of your cellular network. If you can't find Wi-Fi, you can roam on your cellular network. When you're done, avoid further charges by disabling "data roaming" or "cellular data" in your settings.

Save bandwidth-gobbling tasks (Skyping, downloading apps, streaming) for when you're on Wi-Fi.

Use calling/messaging apps for cheaper calls and texts. Some apps (Skype, Viber, FaceTime, Google+ Hangouts) let you call or text for free or cheap.

Use a European SIM card. This option helps you get faster data connections and make voice calls at cheap local rates. Either buy a basic phone in Europe (about $40 from mobile-phone shops) or bring an "unlocked" US phone. In Europe, buy a SIM card to insert in your phone, giving you a European phone number. Buy a new card when you arrive in a new country (sold at phone shops, newsstands, vending machines, and department-store electronics counters).

Finding Wi-Fi in London

Most hotels offer free or cheap Internet access—either a shared computer in the lobby or Wi-Fi in the room. It's smart to get a free account with "The Cloud," a free Wi-Fi service available in many London train stations, museums, cafés, and shopping centers. Sign up at www.thecloud.net/free-wifi (when asked for a local address, I use the Queen's: Buckingham Palace, SW1A 1AA). Tube stations and trains have Wi-Fi—it's free to those with a British Virgin Media account or £2 per day (sign up at http://my.virginmedia.com/wifi). Even without paying, the Tube's Wi-Fi always lets you access Transport for London's helpful Journey Planner (www.tfl.gov.uk), with its real-time updates on delays.

SIGHTSEEING TIPS

Sightseeing Passes: The London Pass, which covers many big sights and lets you skip some lines, is expensive but potentially worth the investment for extremely busy sightseers. Think through your sightseeing plans, study their website to see what's covered, and do the math before you buy (www.londonpass.com).

Avoiding Lines with Advance Tickets: At some sights, you can skip ticket-buying lines by buying in advance online, or with "Fast Track" tickets (sometimes called "priority pass" tickets) purchased at London's TIs, souvenir stands, and travel agencies. Advance tickets can make sense for the Tower of London, London Eye, The Shard, and Madame Tussauds.

Hours: Hours of sights can change unexpectedly; confirm the latest times on the sight's website or visitlondon.com. Many sights stop admitting people 30-60 minutes before closing time, and guards start shooing people out before the actual closing time, so don't save the best for last.

What to Expect: A few important sights, such as the Halls of Parliament, have metal detectors or conduct bag searches that will slow your entry. Others may require you to check (for free) daypacks and coats. Photos and videos are normally allowed, but flashes or tripods usually are not. Many sights offer guided tours and rent audioguides (£5). Most have an on-site café. Expect changes—artwork can be in restoration, displayed elsewhere, or on tour.

Affording London's Sights: Many high-power sights—the British Museum, British Library, National Gallery, and so on—are completely free, but I make a point to donate: It's a great way to get rid of loose change. Many sights offer "concessions" (or "concs") for seniors, children, families, and students—ask. Certain One-Day Travelcards come with discounts at the Churchill War Rooms, Tower of London, and Madame Tussauds (get details at www.daysoutguide.co.uk).

Late Hours: At least one London sight is open late every night, to extend your sightseeing day. ✪ See the sidebar on page 136.

🎧 **Free Rick Steves Audio Tours:** I've produced free audio tours of many of London's best sights, including the British Museum, British Library, St. Paul's Cathedral, The City, and the Westminster neighborhood. You can download Rick Steves Audio Europe via Apple's App Store, Google Play, or the Amazon Appstore.

Theft and Emergencies

Theft: While violent crime is rare in the city center, the Artful Dodger is alive and well in London. Be on guard against pickpockets, particularly on public transportation and in places crowded with tourists. I wear a money belt. Dial 999 for the police. To replace a passport, file a police report, and then call your embassy to make an appointment.

Medical Help: Dial 999 for a medical emergency. For minor ailments, do as the Brits do and go to a pharmacist (a "chemist"), where qualified technicians routinely diagnose and prescribe. Or ask at your hotel for help; they know of the nearest medical and emergency services. Local hospitals

A money belt tucks inside your pants.   The London theater scene rivals Broadway.

have good-quality 24-hour emergency care centers where any tourist can drop in. St. Thomas's Hospital, immediately across the river from Big Ben, has a fine reputation.

ACTIVITIES

Nightlife and Entertainment

London bubbles with top-notch entertainment seven days a week: plays, movie premieres, concerts, Gilbert and Sullivan, tango lessons, stand-up, lectures, Baha'i meetings, walking tours, shopping, museums open late, and the endlessly entertaining pub scene. Perhaps your best entertainment is just to take the Tube to Leicester Square on a pleasant evening, and explore the bustling West End. The two best sources for what's on are *Time Out London* (www.timeout.com/London) and the TI's free monthly *London Planner*.

Theater (a.k.a. "Theatre")

London's theater rivals Broadway's in quality and sometimes beats it in price. Choose from 200 offerings—Shakespeare, glitzy musicals, sex farces, serious chamber drama, cutting-edge fringe, revivals starring movie celebs, and more. London does it all well. Along with the trendiest plays, you'll always find a number of well-executed perennials: *Phantom of the Opera, Les Misérables, The Lion King,* and so on. Most theaters are found in the West End, between Piccadilly and Covent Garden, especially along Shaftesbury Avenue. You'll see the latest offerings advertised all over the

Tube and elsewhere. The free *Official London Theatre Guide* is a handy tool (find it at hotels, box offices, and online at officiallondontheatre.co.uk).

Buying Tickets: Performances are generally every night except Sunday, usually with one or two matinees a week. Tickets range from about £25 to £120. Buy in person from the theater box office (no fee) or online at the theater's website (£3 fee). Often, a theater will reroute you to a third-party ticket vendor such as Ticketmaster. Ticket agencies, located in offices around London, can be convenient but generally charge a 25 percent fee above the face value. Beware of scalpers.

The famous half-price "tkts" booth at Leicester Square sells discounted tickets (25-50 percent off); the best deals are for same-day shows (booth open Mon-Sat 10:00-19:00, Sun 11:00-16:30). Lines often form early, and there's a £3 service charge. Half-price tickets can be a good deal, unless you want the cheapest (balcony) seats or the hottest shows. Check the day's list of available shows at www.tkts.co.uk.

Cheap Tricks: Most theaters offer discounted tickets, called "concessions," or "concs." These can be for matinee performances, standing-room, restricted view seats (behind a pillar), senior/student deals, or tickets returned at the last minute. Buying from scalpers on the street can, like anywhere, get you a good deal or a worthless forgery. Many theaters are so small that there's hardly a bad seat. Bold theatergoers buy cheap tickets, then—as the lights begin to dim—scoot up to a better seat. You wouldn't be the only one rustling in the dark. Shakespeare did it.

Shakespeare's Globe: The Globe (on the South Bank) presents plays from late April through early October in a thatched, open-air replica of the Bard's original theater (as well as year-round performances indoors). The £5 "groundling" tickets—standing-room at the foot of the stage—are most fun (£20-45 to sit, tel. 020/7401-9919, www.shakespearesglobe.com).

Other Performances

Concerts at Historic Churches: Check for free-or-cheap classical music offered many weekdays around 13:00 (www.timeout.com/london). Popular venues are St. Bride's Church (Tube: St. Paul's, www.stbrides.com), St. James's at Piccadilly (Tube: Piccadilly, www.st-james-piccadilly.org), and St. Martin-in-the-Fields on Trafalgar Square (www.smitf.org). St. Martin-in-the-Fields also hosts fine evening concerts by candlelight and Wednesday jazz. Evensong services are held at St. Paul's Cathedral, Westminster Abbey, Southwark Cathedral, and St. Bride's Church.

Opera and Dance: Some of the world's best opera is belted out at the prestigious Royal Opera House, near Covent Garden (www.roh.org.uk), and at the London Coliseum near Leicester Square (English National Opera, www.eno.org). The critically acclaimed Royal Ballet—where Margot Fonteyn and Rudolf Nureyev forged their famous partnership—is based at the Royal Opera House (www.roh.org.uk). Sadler's Wells Theatre features international and UK-based dance troupes (Tube: Angel, www.sadlerswells.com).

Jazz: Ronnie Scott's is London's oldest, and by far most famous, jazz venue, hosting performances daily (47 Frith Street, Tube: Tottenham Court Road or Leicester Square, www.ronniescotts.co.uk).

Seasonal London

Summer Fun: There are plays under the stars at leafy Regent's Park (Tube: Baker Street, www.openairtheatre.org). Royal Albert Hall hosts "Promenade" classical music concerts, known as "Proms," where peasants can score cheap standing-room tickets (Tube: South Kensington, www.bbc.co.uk/proms).

On the South Bank, stroll the Jubilee Walkway along the Thames, from the London Eye to Tower Bridge, past pubs and cafés, the British Film Institute Southbank cinema (tel. 020/7928-3232, check www.bfi.org.uk for schedules), and Shakespeare's Globe. The Scoop, an outdoor amphitheater next to City Hall and Tower Bridge hosts outdoor movies, concerts, dance, and theater—almost nightly and usually free (www.morelondon.com).

Winter Diversions: From late November to early January, London is dressed in its Victorian Christmas best. Trafalgar Square erects a Christmas tree, and outdoor ice rinks emerge at Somerset House and the Tower of London (rental skates available). Store windows glitter along Oxford Street, Bond Street, Regent Street, and Brompton Road. Father Christmas is in his grotto at Harrods (Tube: Knightsbridge) and Selfridges (Tube: Bond Street). Hyde Park stages a kitschy carnival (www.hydeparkwinterwonderland.com). Take in a family-fun holiday play called a "panto," or pantomime (try www.hackneyempire.co.uk or www.oldvictheatre.com). On the South Bank, nibble your way through Christmas markets at the Borough Market (Tube: London Bridge) or the German-flavored Market (Tube: Waterloo, www.xmas-markets.com). Finally, join thousands of revelers on Trafalgar Square to watch fireworks from the London Eye to ring in the New Year.

Tours

▲▲▲Hop-On, Hop-Off Double-Decker Bus Tours: London is full of hop-on, hop-off bus companies competing for your tourist pound. These once-over-lightly bus tours drive by all the famous sights, providing a stress-free way to get your bearings and see the biggies. With a good guide, decent traffic, and nice weather, I'd sit back and enjoy the entire tour. (If traffic is bad or you don't like your guide, you can hop off and try your luck with the next departure.) Each company offers at least one route with live (English-only) guides, and a second (sometimes slightly different route) with recorded, dial-a-language narration. Pick up brochures or check online for the various options, extras, and discounts.

Big Bus London Tours tend to have more frequent buses (£32, up to 30 percent discount online, bigbustours.com). Original **London Sightseeing Bus Tour** is cheaper (£30, £4 Rick Steves discount for two with this book, www.theoriginaltour.com). **See London by Night** offers an atmospheric twilight circuit (£19, tel. 020/7183-4744, www.seelondon bynight.com).

▲▲Walking Tours: Top-notch local guides lead (sometimes big) groups on tours through specific slices of London's past. To take a walking tour, simply show up at the announced location and pay the guide (usually cash only), then enjoy two chatty hours of Dickens, Harry Potter, the Plague, Shakespeare, street art, the Beatles, Jack the Ripper, or whatever is on the agenda. To see what's available, look for brochures, check *Time Out,* or contact the various companies directly. **London Walks** has a wide and fascinating repertoire of tours led by professional guides and actors (£10, tel. 020/7624-3978, recorded info 020/7624-9255, www.walks.com).

Sample sights on a hop-on, hop-off bus tour.

Great local guides make sights come alive.

Practicalities

Sandemans New London has a free, irreverent, youth-oriented tour of the basic sights (tours are "free," but a tip is definitely expected, www.newlondon-tours.com).

Private Guides: Standard rates for registered Blue Badge guides are about £150-165 for four hours, and £240 or more for nine hours (tel. 020/7611-2545, www.guidelondon.org.uk or www.britainsbestguides.org). For a personal guide who can also drive you around London (£500/day), try www.seeitinstyle.synthasite.com.

Bike Tours: Though London traffic is pretty intense to navigate on your own, consider a guided bike tour. **London Bicycle Tour Company** rents to individuals (£3.50/hour, £20/day) and leads tours (£24, includes bike) on three different routes (located at 1a Gabriel's Wharf on the South Bank, Tube: Waterloo, tel. 020/7928-6838, www.londonbicycle.com). **Fat Tire Bike Tours** offers two different itineraries (£22-28, £2 discount with this book, mobile 078-8233-8779, www.fattirebiketourslondon.com).

▲▲**Thames Cruises:** Several boat companies ply the Thames, useful for either a relaxing guided cruise or for point-A-to-B travel around London. The cost varies with the company and destination, but figure around £10 for a one-way ticket across town (£13 round-trip) or £19 for an all-day pass. Buy tickets at the docks. Some companies give discounts if you show your Travelcard or Oyster card, and for children and seniors—it's worth asking.

The handiest boats leave from Westminster Pier (near Big Ben) and Waterloo Pier (near the London Eye). Some helpful stops for sightseers are: Bankside (Shakespeare's Globe), Blackfriars (St. Paul's), London Bridge, and Tower of London. Farther afield, boats go to Greenwich and the Docklands (to the east), and Kew Gardens and Hampton Court to the west.

From Westminster Pier, **City Cruises** is handy to the Tower of London and Greenwich (www.citycruises.com), as is the similar **Thames River Services** (fewer stops, classic boats, www.thamesriverservices.co.uk) and **Circular Cruise** (operated by **Crown River Services,** www.crownrivercruise.co.uk).

From Waterloo Pier, **Thames Clippers** is more like an express commuter bus than a tour cruise, traveling fast and making all the stops along the way (www.thamesclippers.com).

Shopping

London is great for shoppers—and, thanks to the high prices, perhaps even better for window-shoppers. In the 1960s, London set the tone for Mod clothing, and it's been a major fashion capital ever since. If all you need are souvenirs, London's museums generally have bookstores with plenty of small, delightful gift items.

Most stores are open Monday through Saturday from roughly 10:00 to 18:00, and many close Sundays. Large department stores stay open until 21:00. For one-stop shopping for essential items, try large chain stores such as Marks & Spencer.

West End High Fashion: You'll find big-name fashion stores along Regent Street (between Oxford Circus and Piccadilly), old-fashioned gentlemen's stores on Jermyn Street, bookstores along Charing Cross Road, and more boutiques around Covent Garden. All these are part of the West End Walk (✪ see page 61).

Harrods and "Harvey Nick's": Near Hyde Park, you'll find London's most famous and touristy department store, Harrods. With more than four acres of retail space covering seven floors, it has everything from elephants to toothbrushes. Harrods' Georgian Restaurant serves an elegant afternoon tea. The store is also known for its memorial to the late Princess Diana (at the Egyptian Escalator, center of store). The nearby Beauchamp Place is lined with classy and fascinating shops (Mon-Sat 10:00-21:00, Sun 11:30-18:00, located on Brompton Road, Tube: Knightsbridge, tel. 020/7730-1234, www.harrods.com).

A few blocks away is Harvey Nichols. Once Princess Diana's favorite (and now serving Kate Middleton), "Harvey Nick's" remains the department store *du jour* (Mon-Sat 10:00-20:00, Sun 11:30-18:00, near Harrods, 109-125 Knightsbridge, Tube: Knightsbridge, tel. 020/7235-5000, harveynichols.com).

Street Markets: London's weekend flea markets are legendary, and there are early-morning produce markets any day of the week. Covent Garden's daily market is handy to other sightseeing (daily 10:30-18:00, tel. 020/7395-1350, www.coventgardenlife.com).

Portobello Road Market is the classic London street market. On Saturdays, this funky-yet-quaint Notting Hill street of pastel-painted houses and offbeat antiques shops is enlivened even more with 2,000 additional stalls. Antiques, produce, garage-sale items, food stands, live music, and huge crowds create a festival atmosphere. On non-Saturdays, the street itself is fun to explore. (The market is Sat 9:00-19:00, on Sun everything is closed, Tube: Notting Hill Gate, tel. 020/7727-7684, www.portobelloroad.co.uk.)

Camden Lock Market in north London is a huge, trendy, youth-oriented arts-and-crafts festival. It runs daily 10:00-18:00, but is busiest on weekends (Tube: Camden Town, 020/3763-9999, www.camdenlockmarket.com).

For a pleasant Sunday in the East End, take the Tube to Liverpool Street and visit the huge, covered Spitalfields Market (shops open daily until 17:00, www.visitspitalfields.com). Then walk to the Petticoat Lane Market, where a line of stalls sits on the otherwise dull, glass-skyscraper-filled Middlesex Street; adjoining Wentworth Street is more characteristic (best on Sun).

Auction Houses: London's famous auctioneers welcome the curious public Monday through Friday for viewing and bidding. Contact Sotheby's (34 New Bond Street, Tube: Oxford Circus, tel. 020/7293-5000, www.sothebys.com) or Christie's (8 King Street, Tube: Green Park, tel. 020/7839-9060, www.christies.com).

Getting a VAT Refund: If you spend a significant amount on goods at a single store, you may be eligible to get a refund of the 20 percent Value-Added Tax (VAT). The amount varies by retailer—Harrods, for example, won't process a refund unless you spend at least £50. Have the store fill out the paperwork; then, at the airport, get it stamped by Customs and processed by a VAT refund company (at Heathrow, Travelex counters and customs desks are located before and after security in terminals 2-5). Get more details from your merchant or see www.ricksteves.com/vat.

Customs for American Shoppers: You are allowed to take home $800 worth of items per person duty-free, once every 31 days. You can also bring in duty-free a liter of alcohol. As for food, you can take home

One of London's produce markets

Historic red buses still ply some routes.

many processed and packaged foods (e.g., vacuum-packed cheeses, chocolate, mustard) but no fresh produce or meats. Any liquid-containing foods must be packed in checked luggage, a potential recipe for disaster. To check customs rules and duty rates, visit www.help.cbp.gov.

RESOURCES FROM RICK STEVES

This Pocket guide is one of dozens of guidebooks in my series on European travel. I also produce a public television series, *Rick Steves' Europe,* and a public radio show, *Travel with Rick Steves.* My website, www.ricksteves. com, offers a wealth of free travel information, including videos and podcasts of my shows and classes, audio tours of Europe's great sights, travel forums, guidebook updates, my travel blog, and my guide to European rail passes—plus an online travel store and information on our tours of Europe.

How Was Your Trip? If you'd like to share your tips, concerns, and discoveries after using this book, please fill out the survey at ricksteves. com/feedback. It helps us and fellow travelers. Cheers!

British-Yankee Vocabulary

afters—dessert

anticlockwise—counterclockwise

bangers and mash—sausage and mashed potatoes

bloody—damn

blow off—fart

bobby—policeman ("the Bill" is more common)

Bob's your uncle—there you go (with a shrug), naturally

boffin—nerd, geek

bollocks—testicles (used in many colorful expressions)

bolshy—argumentative

bubble and squeak—cabbage and potatoes fried together

bum—butt

cheers—good-bye or thanks; also a toast

chemist—pharmacist

chippie—fish-and-chip shop; carpenter (see also "joiner")

chock-a-block—jam-packed

chuffed—pleased

concs (pronounced "conks")—short for "concession," or discount

crisps—potato chips

cuppa—cup of tea

curry—any Indian meal flavored with curry, popular with all Brits

dear—expensive

donkey's years—ages, long time

dummy—pacifier

elevenses—coffee-and-biscuits break before lunch

fag—cigarette

fagged—exhausted

faggot—meatball

fairy cake—cupcake

fancy—to like, to be attracted to (a person)

fanny—vagina

first floor—second floor

fizzy drink—pop or soda

flat—apartment

Frogs—French people

full Monty—whole shebang; everything

geezer—dude (slang for young man)

green fingers—green thumbs

grizzle—grumble, fuss (especially by a baby)

gutted—deeply disappointed

half eight—8:30 (not 7:30)

hash sign—pound sign, as on a phone

hen night—bachelorette party

holiday—vacation

homely—homey or cozy

ice lolly—Popsicle

Joe Bloggs—John Q. Public

jumble sale—rummage sale

just a tick—just a second

knackered—exhausted (Cockney: cream crackered)

knickers—ladies' panties

ladybird—ladybug

left luggage—baggage check

let—rent, as in property

licenced—restaurant authorized to sell alcohol

lie-in, having a—sleeping in late

lift—elevator

loo—toilet or bathroom

lorry—truck

mac—mackintosh raincoat

Marmite—yeast paste, spread on sandwiches

mate—buddy (boy or girl)

mews—former stables converted to two-story rowhouses (London)

moggie—cat

naff—dorky

natter—talk on and on

noughts & **crosses**—tic-tac-toe

off-licence—liquor store

on offer—for sale

pants—underwear, briefs

pear-shaped—messed up, gone wrong

petrol—gas

pissed, **paralytic**, **bevvied**, **wellied**, **popped up**, **merry**, **trollied**, **ratted**, **rat-arsed**, **pissed as a newt**—drunk

public school—private "prep" school (e.g., Eton)

pudding—dessert in general

pull, to be on the—looking for love

punter—customer, especially in gambling

quid—a pound (money)

randy—horny

ring up—call (telephone)

rubber—eraser

rubbish—bad

serviette—napkin

shag—intercourse (cruder than in the US)

smalls—underwear

snogging—kissing, making out

sod—mildly offensive insult

sod it, sod off—screw it, screw off

spend a penny—urinate

stag night—bachelor party

starkers—buck naked

stone—14 pounds (weight)

stroppy—bad-tempered

subway—underground walkway

ta—thank you

tatty—worn out or tacky

telly—TV

tenner—£10 bill

tight as a fish's bum—cheapskate (watertight)

top hole—first rate

top up—refill a drink

torch—flashlight

twee—quaint, cute

twitcher—bird watcher

way out—exit

wee (adj)—small (Scottish)

Wellingtons, wellies—rubber boots

whacked—exhausted

whinge (rhymes with hinge)—whine

wind up—tease, irritate

witter on—gab and gab

yob—hooligan

zed—the letter Z

INDEX

PHOTO CREDITS

Start your trip at

Our website enhances this book and turns

Explore Europe

At ricksteves.com you can browse through thousands of articles, videos, photos and radio interviews, plus find a wealth of money-saving travel tips for planning your dream trip. And with our mobile-friendly website, you can easily access all this great travel information anywhere you go.

TV Shows

Preview the places you'll visit by watching entire half-hour episodes of Rick Steves' Europe (choose from all 100 shows) on-demand, for free.

ricksteves.com

your travel dreams into affordable reality

Radio Interviews

Enjoy ready access to Rick's vast library of radio interviews covering  travel tips and cultural insights that relate specifically to your Europe travel plans.

Travel Forums

Learn, ask, share! Our online community of savvy travelers is a great resource for first-time travelers to Europe, as well as seasoned pros. You'll find forums on each country, plus travel tips and restaurant/hotel reviews. You can even ask one of our well-traveled staff to chime in with an opinion.

Travel News

Subscribe to our free Travel News e-newsletter, and get monthly updates from Rick on what's happening in Europe.

Audio Europe™

Rick's Free Travel App

Get your FREE Rick Steves Audio Europe™ app to enjoy...

- Dozens of self-guided tours of Europe's top museums, sights and historic walks
- Hundreds of tracks filled with cultural insights and sightseeing tips from Rick's radio interviews
- All organized into handy geographic playlists
- For Apple and Android

With Rick whispering in your ear, Europe gets even better.

Find out more at ricksteves.com

Pack Light and Right

Gear up for your next adventure at ricksteves.com

Light Luggage

Pack light and right with Rick Steves' affordable, custom-designed rolling carry-on bags, backpacks, day packs and shoulder bags.

Accessories

From packing cubes to moneybelts and beyond, Rick has personally selected the travel goodies that will help your trip go smoother.

Shop at ricksteves.com

Rick Steves has

Experience maximum Europe

Save time and energy

This guidebook is your independent-travel toolkit. But for all it delivers, it's still up to you to devote the time and energy it takes to manage the preparation and logistics that are essential for a happy trip. If that's a hassle, there's a solution.

Rick Steves Tours

A Rick Steves tour takes you to Europe's most interesting places with great guides and small groups

great tours, too!

with minimum stress

of 28 or less. We follow Rick's favorite itineraries, ride in comfy buses, stay in family-run hotels, and bring you intimately close to the Europe you've traveled so far to see. Most importantly, we take away the logistical headaches so you can focus on the fun.

Join the fun

This year we'll take thousands of free-spirited travelers—nearly half of them repeat customers—along with us on four dozen different itineraries, from Ireland to Italy to Istanbul. Is a Rick Steves tour the right fit for your travel dreams? Find out at ricksteves.com, where you can also request Rick's latest tour catalog.

Europe is best experienced with happy travel partners. We hope you can join us.

See our itineraries at ricksteves.com

A Guide for Every Trip

BEST OF GUIDES

Full color easy-to-scan format, focusing on Europe's most popular destinations and sights.

Best of England
Best of Europe
Best of France
Best of Germany
Best of Ireland
Best of Italy
Best of Spain

COMPREHENSIVE GUIDES

City, country, and regional guides with detailed coverage for a multi-week trip exploring iconic sights and more.

Amsterdam & the Netherlands
Barcelona
Belgium: Bruges, Brussels, Antwerp & Ghent
Berlin
Budapest
Croatia & Slovenia
Eastern Europe
England
Florence & Tuscany
France
Germany
Great Britain
Greece: Athens & the Peloponnese
Iceland
Ireland
Istanbul
Italy
London
Paris
Portugal
Prague & the Czech Republic
Provence & the French Riviera
Rome
Scandinavia
Scotland
Spain
Switzerland
Venice
Vienna, Salzburg & Tirol

Rick Steves guidebooks are published by Avalon Travel, an imprint of Perseus Books, a Hachette Book Group company.

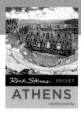

Rick Steves POCKET
AMSTERDAM

Rick Steves POCKET
ATHENS

Rick Steves POCKET
BARCELONA

Rick Steves POCKET
LONDON

POCKET GUIDES

SNAPSHOT GUIDES

Focused single-destination coverage.

CRUISE PORTS GUIDES

Reference for cruise ports of call.

TRAVEL SKILLS & CULTURE

PHRASE BOOKS & DICTIONARIES

PLANNING MAPS

Rick Steves books are available from your favorite bookseller.
Many guides are available as ebooks.

Avalon Travel
An imprint of Perseus Books
A Hachette Book Group company
1700 Fourth Street
Berkeley, CA 94710

Printed in China by RR Donnelley.
Third Edition
Second printing June 2018.

ISBN 978-1-63121-561-2
ISSN 2159-6794

For the latest on Rick's lectures, books, tours, public radio show, and public television
series, contact Rick Steves' Europe, 130 Fourth Avenue North, Edmonds, WA 98020,
tel. 425/771-8303, ricksteves.com, rick@ricksteves.com.

Rick Steves' Europe
Managing Editor: Jennifer Madson Davis
Special Publications Manager: Risa Laib
Editors: Glenn Eriksen, Tom Griffin, Katherine Gustafson, Suzanne Kotz, Cathy Lu,
John Pierce, Carrie Shepherd
Editorial & Production Assistant: Jessica Shaw
Editorial Intern: Megan Simms
Researcher: Robyn Stencil
Graphic Content Director: Sandra Hundacker
Maps & Graphics: David C. Hoerlein, Lauren Mills, Mary Rostad

Avalon Travel
Senior Editor and Series Manager: Madhu Prasher
Editor: Jamie Andrade
Associate Editor: Sierra Machado
Copy Editor: Kelly Lydick
Proofreader: Becca Freed
Indexer: Stephen Callahan
Production & Typesetting: Tabitha Lahr
Cover Design: Kimberly Glyder Design
Interior Design: Darren Alessi
Maps and Graphics: Kat Bennett
Cover Photo: Tower Bridge © Tomas1111 | Dreamstime.com

ABOUT THE AUTHORS

Rick Steves

Since 1973, Rick has spent about four months a year exploring Europe. His mission: to empower Americans to have European trips that are fun, affordable, and culturally broadening. Rick produces a best-selling guidebook series, a public television series, and a public radio show, and organizes small-group tours that take over 20,000 travelers to Europe annually. He does all of this with the help of a hardworking, well-traveled staff of 100 at Rick Steves' Europe in Edmonds, Washington, near Seattle. When not on the road, Rick is active in his church and with advocacy groups focused on economic justice, drug policy reform, and ending hunger. To recharge, Rick plays piano, relaxes at his family cabin in the Cascade Mountains, and spends time with his partner Trish, son Andy, and daughter Jackie. Find out more about Rick at www.ricksteves.com and on Facebook.

Gene Openshaw

Gene has co-authored a dozen Rick Steves books, specializing in writing walks and tours of Europe's cities, museums, and cultural sights. He also contributes to Rick's public television series, produces tours for Rick Steves Audio Europe, and is a regular guest on Rick's public radio show. Outside of the travel world, Gene has co-authored *The Seattle Joke Book.* As a composer, Gene has written a full-length opera called *Matter* (soundtrack available on Amazon), a violin sonata, and dozens of songs. He lives near Seattle with his daughter, enjoys giving presentations on art and history, and roots for the Mariners in good times and bad.

FOLDOUT COLOR MAP

The foldout map on the opposite page includes:
- A map of London on one side
- Maps of London's neighborhoods, bus routes, train stations, selected sites, and the London Underground on the other side